McGraw-Hill Ryerson

Foundations of Mathematics 10

STUDENT WORKBOOK

1ST EDITION

Author
Ken Stewart
B.Sc. (Hons.), B.Ed.
York Region District School Board

Reviewer
Wayne Erdman
B. Math., B.Ed.
Toronto District School Board

McGraw-Hill
Ryerson

McGraw-Hill Ryerson
Toronto   Montréal   Boston   Burr Ridge, IL   Dubuque, IA   Madison, WI   New York
San Francisco   St. Louis   Bangkok   Bogotá   Caracas   Kuala Lumpur   Lisbon   London
Madrid   Mexico City   Milan   New Delhi   Santiago   Seoul   Singapore   Sydney   Taipei

The McGraw·Hill Companies

McGraw-Hill Ryerson

COPIES OF THIS BOOK
MAY BE OBTAINED BY
CONTACTING:

McGraw-Hill Ryerson Ltd.

WEB SITE:
www.mcgrawhill.ca

E-MAIL:
orders@mcgrawhill.ca

TOLL-FREE FAX:
1-800-463-5885

TOLL-FREE CALL:
1-800-565-5758

OR BY MAILING YOUR
ORDER TO:
McGraw-Hill Ryerson
Order Department
300 Water Street
Whitby, ON L1N 9B6

Please quote the ISBN and
title when placing your
order.

Student Resource ISBN:
978-0-07-097768-6

McGraw-Hill Ryerson
Foundations of Mathematics 10
Student Workbook
1ˢᵗ Edition

ISBN-13: 978-0-07-000273-9
ISBN-10: 0-07-000273-8

www.mcgrawhill.ca

5 6 7 8 9 10 MP 1 9 8 7

Printed and bound in Canada

Care has been taken to trace ownership of copyright material contained in this text. The
publishers will gladly accept any information that will enable them to rectify any reference
or credit in subsequent printings.

Publisher: Linda Allison
Associate Mathematics Publisher: Kristi Clark
Project Manager: Pronk & Associates
Developmental Editing: Pronk&Associates; Write On!
Manager, Editorial Services: Crystal Shortt
Supervising Editor: Christine Arnold
Copy Editing: Write On!
Editorial Assistant: Erin Hartley
Review Coordinator: Jennifer Keay
Manager, Production Services: Yolanda Pigden
Production Co-ordinator: Zonia Strynatka
Cover Design: Liz Harasymczuk
Interior Design: Valid Design & Layout
Electronic Page Make-Up: Valid Design & Layout
Cover Image: Courtesy of Getty Images

Contents

CHAPTER 1

Measurement Systems and Similar Triangles

CHAPTER 2

Right Triangle Trigonometry

CHAPTER 3

Linear Relations

CHAPTER 4

Linear Equations

Features of This Workbook

Warm-Up Guide
This two-page guide lists hints and techniques to help you answer the **Warm-Up** questions at the beginning of each numbered section.

Succeed on the Chapter Tests
This section outlines a number of methods you can use to study more effectively and improve your results on the chapter tests.

Get Set
At the beginning of each chapter, a page of questions reviews key skills from other mathematics courses and from previous chapters.

Numbered Sections

Warm-Up
Each section starts with six to eight **Warm-Up** questions, which provide an ongoing review of the major topics of the course. Often, these questions include prerequisite skills for the next topic.

Practise
The **Practise** pages give you a chance to apply and extend the concepts you have just learned. Often, the first questions outline the steps in the solution to help you understand the mathematics used to answer the question. Then, you advance to answering similar questions without guidance.

Chapter Review
The **Chapter Review** has a set of questions covering all the numbered sections in the chapter. As you work through these questions, you can identify the topics for which more study and practice will help you do your best on the chapter test.

CHAPTER 1

Measurement Systems and Similar Triangles

Get Set

Answer these questions to check your understanding of the Get Ready concepts on pages 4–5 of the *Foundations of Mathematics 10* textbook.

Fraction and Number Sense

1. Order the numbers in each set from least to greatest.

a) $\dfrac{1}{2}, \dfrac{1}{12}, \dfrac{1}{4}, \dfrac{1}{8}$

$\dfrac{1}{12} < \dfrac{1}{8} < \dfrac{1}{4} < \dfrac{1}{2}$

b) $1\dfrac{1}{2}, 2\dfrac{3}{8}, \dfrac{17}{8}, 1\dfrac{3}{4}, 2\dfrac{1}{4}$

$1\dfrac{1}{2} < 1\dfrac{3}{4} < \dfrac{7}{8} < 2\dfrac{1}{4} < 2\dfrac{3}{8}$

c) $\dfrac{1}{2}, \dfrac{1}{5}, \dfrac{1}{3}, \dfrac{1}{6}$

$\dfrac{1}{6} < \dfrac{1}{5} < \dfrac{1}{3} < \dfrac{1}{2}$

2. Simplify. Express your answers in lowest terms.

a) $\dfrac{2}{3} + \dfrac{3}{4}$

$= \dfrac{8}{12} + \dfrac{9}{12}$

$= \dfrac{17}{12}$

b) $\dfrac{1}{8} \times 2$

$= \dfrac{1}{4}$

c) $27 \div \dfrac{1}{3}$

$= 27 \times 3$

$= 81$

d) $1\dfrac{1}{2} + 2\dfrac{3}{4}$

$= \dfrac{3}{2} + \dfrac{11}{4}$

$= \dfrac{6}{4} + \dfrac{11}{4}$

$= \dfrac{17}{4}$

Ratio and Proportion

3. Write each ratio in simplest form.

a) 2:4

$= 1:2$

b) 18:6

$= 3:1$

c) 54:45

$= 6:5$

d) 22:121

$= 2:11$

4. Solve.

a) $\dfrac{m}{2} = \dfrac{3}{4}$

$4m = 6$

$m = \dfrac{6}{4}$

$m = \dfrac{3}{2}$

b) $y:15 = 4:60$

$60y = 60$

$y = 1$

c) $3:2 = t:22$

$2t = 66$

$t = 33$

d) $2.5:x = 10:84$

$10x = 210$

$x = 21$

Angle Properties

5. Find the measure of each indicated angle.

a)

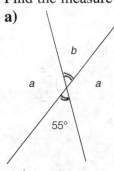

$b = 55°$

$a = 180° - b$

$= 180° - 55°$

$= 125°$

b)

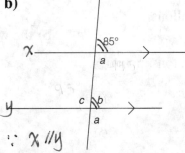

$\because x // y$

$\therefore b = 85°$

$\therefore a = c = 180° - b$

$= 180° - 85°$

$= 95°$

c)

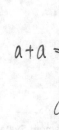

$a + a = 180° - 30° = 160°$ ~~150°~~

$a = 160° \div 2 = 80°$

~~$a = \dfrac{150}{2} = 75°$~~

Date: _____

Textbook
pp. 6–11

Warm-Up

1 ft = 12 inches

1. Units of Measure	2. Number Sense inches
Identify each imperial unit as a measure of length, volume, or weight. **a)** mile → length **b)** pound → weight **c)** inch → length **d)** quart → volume	There are 12 in. in 1 ft. Calculate the number of inches in **a)** 2 ft $2 \times 12 = 24$ in. **b)** 5 ft $5 \times 12 = 60$ in.

3. Mental Math	4. Proportional Reasoning
If 1 yd = 3 ft, then 1 yd² = __9__ ft².	Convert the following: **a)** 5 yd = __15__ ft **b)** __5__ ft = 60 in. **c)** 24 in. = __2__ ft

5. Math Literacy	6. Multiply Fractions

? Give three examples in your everyday life where measurements would be given in the imperial system.
 	
– inches
– pound
– ft
	Simplify.
	a) $8^2 \times \dfrac{3}{4}$
	   = 6
	
	b) $\dfrac{1}{8} \times 24^3$
	   = 3

7. Number Sense	8. Estimation

Circle the imperial units you would use to measure the following:
 	
a) the size of a book: yards, (inches), feet
 	
b) the volume of a glass: gallons, tablespoons, (fluid ounces)
 	
c) the mass of a cat: ounces, tons, (pounds)
 	
b) ounces < pounds < tons
	Use imperial units to estimate each measure.
	a) the height of your classroom door
	   feet
	
	b) the weight of a basketball
	
	   ton

Practise

Use the table

Unit		alent
Fluid ounce		mL
Pint		nL
Quart		nL
Gallon		L

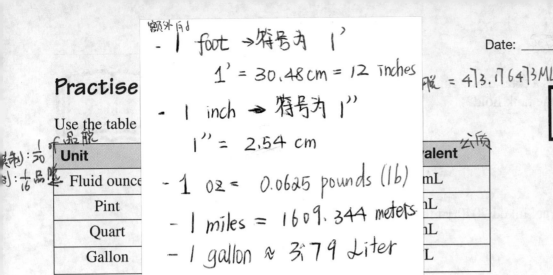

Handwritten notes (overlaid box):
- 1 foot →特号为 1'
  1' = 30.48 cm = 12 inches
- 1 inch → 特号为 1"
  1" = 2.54 cm
- 1 oz = 0.0625 pounds (lb)
- 1 miles = 1609.344 meters
- 1 gallon ≈ 3.79 Liter

额外问 (top left)

= 473.176473ML (top right)

1. Carmella h _____ pt bottles can she fill?

$\frac{7580}{473} \approx 16.03 \approx 1]$

1 pt = 473 mL
2 Gallon = 3.79 × 2 = 7.58L = 7580mL

She can fill 17 bottles.

2. Steve has 6 qt of distilled water. Can he store the water in a 1-gal jug? Explain.

6 × 946mL = 5676 mL

3.79 L = 3790 mL

Yes, but he'll need one more Jug.

Use the table to complete questions 3 to 5.

Length	Mass	Volume
1 ft = 12 in.	1 lb = 16 oz	1 gal = 4 qt
1 yd = 3 ft	1 ton (tn) = 2000 lb	1 qt = 2 pt
1 mi = 1760 yd	1 kg = 2lb	1 pt = 16 fl oz

1 qt = 32 fl oz

(right margin handwritten):
1 foot = 1' = 30.48 cm = 12 Inches
1" = 1 Inches ≈ 2.54 cm

3. Convert each measure to inches.
   a) 3'
   = 3 × 12 = 36 Inches
   b) 2' 7"
   c) 8.5'

4. Convert each measure to feet and inches.
   a) 71 in.
   ≈ 5.92 ft 5'11"
   b) 66 in.
   = 5.5 ft 5'6"
   c) 216 in.
   = 18 ft 18'

1 oz = 0.0625 pound

5. Convert each measure to pounds.
   a) 88 oz
   = 5.5 lb
   b) 2.1 tn
   = 2.1 × 2000 = 4100 lb
   c) 192 oz
   = 192 ÷ 16 = 12 lb

6. The school gymnasium floor needs to be resurfaced. Hardwood flooring costs $6 per square foot plus $2.50 per square foot for installation. The gym measures 180 ft by 220 ft.

① 每平方英尺
② 安装

   a) How large is the gym in square feet?
   180 × 220 = 39600 (square feet)

   b) How much would it cost to buy the hardwood flooring for the gym?
   39600 × 6 = 237600 dollars

   c) How much would it cost to install the hardwood flooring in the gym?
   237600 + 39600 × 2.5 = 237600 + 99000 = 336600 (dollars)
   99000

Date: _____

Section 1.1

7. Ace's car holds a total of 12 gal of gasoline. How many quarts of gasoline will the tank hold?

$12 \times 4 = 48$.

The tank hold 48 quarts of gasoline.

8. Meghan and Paul hiked 7040 yd through the forest to the pond. How far did they hike in miles?

$\dfrac{7040}{1760} = $ 4 miles

9. Eric is 5′ 7″ tall. What would his height be in inches?

5′7″

= 5 ft 7 inches

$5 \times 12 = 60$ inches

$60 + 7 = 67$ inches.

His height be in inches is 67.

10. A $\dfrac{1}{2}$ pt of cream yields 2 c of whipped cream. How many cups of whipped cream would result from whipping $1\dfrac{1}{2}$ pt of cream?

2 cups

$1\dfrac{1}{2} = \dfrac{3}{2} = 3 \times \dfrac{1}{2}$

$3 \times 2 = 6$ ∴ 6 cups

11. Monica is putting a patio in her yard. Patio stones come in squares measuring 1 ft by 1 ft. She wants the patio to be 8 stones wide and 9 stones long.

a) How many square feet will the patio be when Monica is finished?

$8 \times 1 = 8$

$9 \times 1 = 9$

$8 \times 9 = 72$ square feet

b) If the patio stones cost $5.00 each, how much will the patio cost altogether?

$72 \times 5 = \$360$

1.2 Conversions Between Metric and Imperial Systems

Textbook
pp. 12–18

Warm-Up

1. Metric Units of Measure

①公制单位

List the metric units for each.

Length: __meter (m), kilometer (km), centimeters (cm)__

Volume: ~~cubic meter (m³)~~, Litres, millilitres

Mass: __kilograms (kg), gram (g), tonne (t)__

milligrams (mg)

2. Number Sense

Convert each measure using the indicated units.

a) 42 mm   centimetres 4.2 cm
b) 12 kg   grams 12000 g
c) 1.8 m   centimetres 180 cm
d) 2400 m   kilometres 2.4 km
e) 980 mg   grams 0.98 g

3. Estimate

Use an appropriate metric measure to estimate each measure.

a) the length of your finger

6.3 cm

b) the mass of a nickel

2 gram

4. Proportional Reasoning

Convert each measure using the indicated units.

a) 5 qt   = 10 pints
b) 4 ft   = 48 inches
c) 24 oz   = 1.5 pounds
d) 2 yd   = 6   feet
e) 3 gal   = 12 quarts

5. Number Sense

Circle the metric units you would use to measure the following:

a) the length of your shoe: metres, kilometres, (centimetres)

b) the mass of 5 sheets of paper: kilograms, litres, (grams)

克

c) the volume of a pop can: (millilitres,) centimetres, litres

升   毫升

6. Math Literacy

a) Describe a situation in which the metric system of measure is commonly used.

b) Describe a situation in which the imperial system of measure is commonly used.

7. Mental Math

Calculate mentally.
a) 42 × 10 000 = 420000
b) 560 ÷ 100 = 5.6
c) 2458 ÷ 1000 = 2.458
d) 65 × 0.1 = 6.5
e) 425 × 0.01 = 4.25

8. Estimate Measures

Use an appropriate imperial unit to estimate each measure.

a) the temperature in your room
25°C

b) the mass of your math textbook

2 lb

Practise: Metric and Imperial Conversions

Section
1.2

Estimate Temperature Conversions

1. To estimate the Fahrenheit temperature given a temperature in degrees Celsius, double the Celsius temperature, then add 30. Estimate each temperature in degrees Fahrenheit.

a) 22°C

$= 2 \times 22 + 30$
$= 74 \, °F$

b) 53°C

$= 53 \times 2 + 70$
$= 136 \, °F$

c) −24°C

$(-24) \cdot 2 + 30$
$= -48 + 30$
$= -18$

2. To estimate the Celsius temperature for a given temperature in degrees Fahrenheit, subtract 30, then divide by 2. Estimate each temperature in degrees Celsius.

a) 88°F

$\frac{88-30}{2} = 29°C$

b) −20°F

$= \frac{-20-30}{2} = -25°C$

c) 222°F

$= \frac{222-30}{2} = 96°C$

Estimate Metric to Imperial Conversions

Use these benchmarks to answer question 3.

> There are approximately 1.6 km in 1 mi.
> There are approximately 2.5 cm in 1 in.
> One yard is approximately equal to 1 mi.
> There are approximately 450 g in 1 lb.
> There are approximately 2.2 lb in 1 kg.
> There are approximately 4 L in 1 U.S. gallon.
> One tablespoon is approximately equal to 15 mL.
> There are approximately 30 mL in 1 fl oz.

3. a) About how many tablespoons are in 60 mL?

$\frac{60}{15} = 4$ About 4 tablespoons are in 60 mL.

b) About how many pounds are in 2.5 kg?

$2.5 \times 2.2 = 5.5$ pounds

There are about 5.5 pounds in 2.5 kg.

c) About how many centimetres are in 12 in.?

$12 \times 2.5 = 30$ cm

There are about 30 cm in 12 in..

d) About how many millilitres are in 5.5 fl oz?

$30 \times 5.5 = 165$ mL

There are about 165 mL in 5.5 fl oz.

Applying Measurement Conversions

4. To accurately convert degrees Celsius to degrees Fahrenheit, multiply by $\frac{9}{5}$, then add 32.

a) Explain why doubling the Celsius temperature then adding 30 is a good approximation.

— Because $\frac{9}{5}$ is amost double for $\frac{5}{5}$, and add/subtract 30 is easier to add/subtract 32.

b) When can you estimate and when must you be exact?

5. Jaycee's doctor recommends that she drink 2 L of water every day. How many cups of water is this?

6. Water boils at 100°C and freezes at 0°C.

a) Calculate the temperature at which water boils in degrees Fahrenheit.

$100 \times \frac{9}{5} = 180$

$180 + 32 = 212\ °F$

b) Calculate the temperature at which water freezes in degrees Fahrenheit.

$0 \times \frac{9}{5} + 32 = 32\ °F$

7. Jeric and his family are taking a trip to the southern United States this winter break. Driving at an average speed of 50 mi per hour (mph), the trip will take 22 h.

a) Calculate the number of miles to drive one way.

$50 \times 22 = 1100$ miles.

$\frac{23}{110}$

b) Convert the one-way distance from miles to kilometres.

$1100 \times 1609.34 = 1770274$

$1770274 \div 1000 = 1770.274$ km.

c) Find the total distance of the round trip in kilometres.

$1770.274 \times 2 = 3540.548$ km

d) The family car uses 6.3 L of gas per 100 km. How many litres of gas are needed for the round trip?

$\frac{3540.548}{100} \times 6.3 L \approx 35.40548 \times 6.3$

$\approx 35.40 \times 6.3$

$= 223.02 L.$

1.3 Similar Triangles

Textbook
pp. 19–29

Warm-Up

1. Parallel Lines

Which angles have the same measure as ∠a?

∠a = ∠d = ∠e = ∠h

2. Corresponding Angles

Identify the corresponding angles.

∠a = ∠C

∠b = ∠d = ∠e

3. Corresponding Sides

Triangles ABC and DEF are congruent. 全等
Find the lengths of the sides of △ABC.

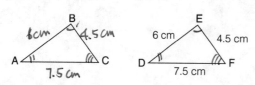

4. Opposite Angles

Name the opposite angles.

∠RST = 120° = ∠QSU

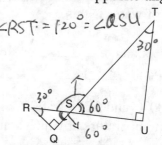

5. Math Literacy

How can you tell if two triangles are congruent?

Each angles are equal and length are the same.

6. Congruent Triangles

Triangles RST and VWX are congruent. Find the measures of ∠S and ∠X.

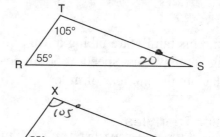

7. Proportions

Solve each proportion.

a) $\dfrac{AB}{5} = \dfrac{12}{15}$

15 AB = 60

AB = 4

b) $\dfrac{4}{16} = \dfrac{LM}{24}$

16 LM = 96

LM = 6

8. Parallel Lines

Name two groups of equal angles.

∠R = ∠4 = ∠K

∠S = ∠V = ∠L

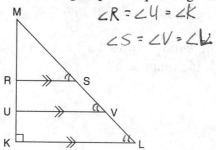

Practise: Corresponding Angles and Corresponding Sides

Section
1.3

1. Given that △PQR ~ △GHI, find the measures of the indicated angles.

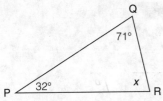

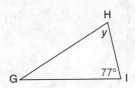

$x = 77°$
$y = 71°$

2. These triangles are similar.

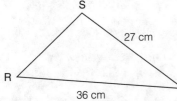

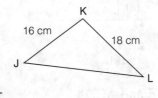

a) Side RS corresponds to _Side JK_, side ST corresponds to _Side KL_ and side RT corresponds to _Side JL_.

b) Complete the proportionality statement:
Since △ _RST_ ~ △ _KJL_, then the lengths of _those two triangles_ _____
are proportional.

c) Find the lengths of the indicated sides.

$$\frac{RS}{JK} = \frac{ST}{KL}$$

$$\frac{RS}{16} = \frac{27}{18}$$

$$RS = \frac{16 \times 27}{18}$$

$$\doteq 24$$

Use Similar Triangles

3. Examine △ABF and △ECF.

a) Are the two triangles similar? How do you know?

Yes. ∠B = ∠C ∴ AB∥CE ∴ ∠A = ∠E. ∴∠BFA = ∠EFC.

b) What is the length of side CE?
Round to one decimal place.

$$\frac{CE}{AB} = \frac{FE}{AF}$$

$$\frac{CE}{3.1} = \frac{2.9}{3.8}$$

$$CE = \frac{3.1 \times 2.9}{3.8}$$

$$\doteq 2.3$$

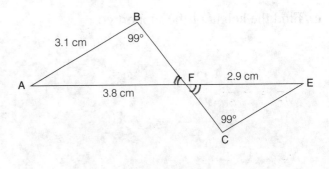

4. A support wire is attached to the ground 45 m from the base of a telecommunications tower. The wire is attached to the tower 30 m up from the ground. A post supports the wire at a point 15 m from the base of the tower.

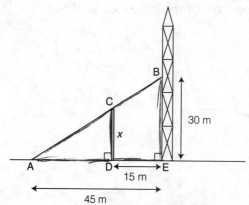

a) Sketch and label triangles ABE and ACD.

$$\triangle ABE \sim \triangle ACD$$

b) Are triangles ABE and ACD similar? How do you know?

Yes.

c) Find the height of the support post.

$$\frac{BE}{CD} = \frac{AE}{AE\text{-}DE}$$

$$= \frac{30}{CD} = \frac{45}{45-15} \qquad x=20$$

$$CD = \frac{30 \times 30}{45}$$

$$CD = 20$$

1.4 Solve Problems Using Similar Triangles

Textbook
pp. 30–37

Warm-Up

1. Similar Triangles

Identify corresponding sides in these similar triangles.

$\triangle DFE \sim \triangle GFH$

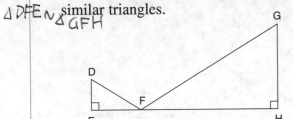

2. Similar Triangles

In similar triangles,

a) how many pairs of sides are

corresponding? ___3___

b) how many pairs of angles are

corresponding? ___3___

3. Solve a Proportion

Calculate the length of AB.

$\dfrac{AB}{15} = \dfrac{5}{3}$

$3AB = 75$

$AB = 25$

4. Math Literacy

Give two real-life examples in which the properties of similar triangles are used.

5. Mental Math

Determine how many times as long the side lengths of Triangle A are compared to those of Triangle B.

$10 \div 2 = 5$
$20 \div 4 = 5$
$15 \div 3 = 5$

$\therefore 5:1$

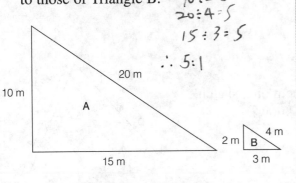

6. Corresponding Angles

Identify the corresponding angles in these similar triangles.

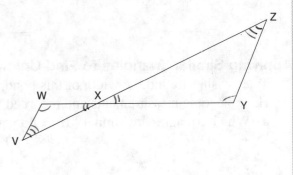

7. Proportions

Solve each proportion.

a) $\dfrac{b}{3} = \dfrac{6}{12}$ $b = \dfrac{18}{12} = 1.5$

b) $\dfrac{8}{18} = \dfrac{m}{27}$ $m = 12$

8. Find a Side Length

Triangles DEF and MNP are similar. Find the length of MN.

$\dfrac{PN}{FE} = \dfrac{15}{12} = \dfrac{5}{4}$

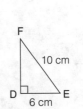
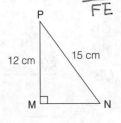

$\overset{3}{\cancel{6}} \times \dfrac{5}{\cancel{4}_2} = \dfrac{15}{2}$ cm

$MN = 7.5$ cm

Practise: Solve Problems Using Similar Triangles

Section 1.4

1. a) Are △ABC and △DEF similar? How do you know?

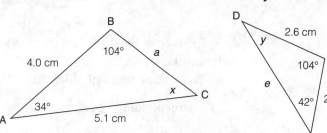

∠B = ∠E

$y = 180° - 104° - 42° = 34° = ∠A$

$x = 180° - 104° - 34° = 42° = ∠F$

∴ ∠ABC ~ △DEF

b) Find the measures of the indicated sides and angles.

Since △ _ABC_ ~ △ _DEF_ , corresponding angles are _____.

Therefore, ∠C = ∠ _F_

= _42_ °

and ∠D = ∠ _A_

= _34_ °

$$\frac{BC}{EF} = \frac{AB}{DE} \qquad \frac{DF}{AC} = \frac{DE}{AB}$$

$$\frac{BC}{2.1} = \frac{4.0}{2.6} \qquad \frac{DF}{5.1} = \frac{2.6}{4.0}$$

$$BC = \frac{2.1 \times 4.0}{2.6} \qquad DF = \frac{5.1 \times 2.6}{4.0}$$

$$\doteq 3.23 \qquad \doteq 3.315$$

Applying Similar Triangles to Find Unknowns

2. Tyler wishes to find the width of this pond.
He took some measurements and recorded them on a sketch. 素描

a) Which triangles are similar? How do you know?

∴ DE∥CB   ∴∠PAE = ∠CAB

∴ ∠AED = ∠ABC

$\frac{AB}{AE} = \frac{32+70}{32} = 3.19$

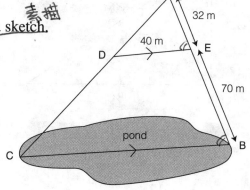

b) How wide is the pond? Give your answer
to the nearest tenth of a metre.

$$\frac{CB}{} = \frac{}{AE}$$

$$\frac{CB}{40} = \frac{}{32}$$

$$CB = \frac{40 \times }{32}$$

$$\doteq \underline{}$$

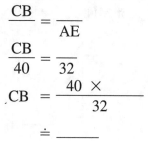

Date: _____

3. On a sunny day in Egypt, a stick is placed vertically so 2 m of it is above ground. The stick casts a shadow 4 m long. At the same time, one of the Great Pyramids of Egypt casts a shadow 179 m long. The shadow of the pyramid is measured from the base of the pyramid. The pyramid is 230 m wide.

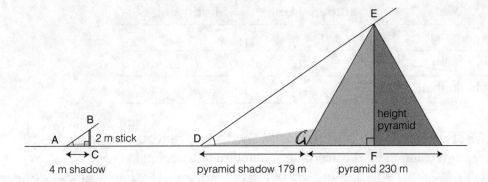

a) Are triangles ABC and DEF similar? How do you know?

$$DG = 179 \text{ cm}$$
$$GF = \frac{230}{2} = 115 \text{ cm}$$

$$\frac{115}{4} = 28.75$$

$$\angle C = \angle EFD$$

b) What is the length of DF?

$$DF = DG + GF = 179 + 115 = 294$$

c) What is the height of the pyramid? Give your answer to the nearest tenth of a metre.

$$\frac{EF}{BC} = \frac{DF}{AC}$$
$$\frac{EF}{2} = \frac{294}{4}$$
$$EF = \frac{2 \times 294}{4}$$
$$= 147$$

Chapter 1 Review

1.1 Imperial Measure, textbook pages 6–11

1. Estimate each measure in imperial and metric units.

Measure	Imperial Units	Metric Units
the temperature in your room	71.6 °F	22°C
the mass of your math textbook	3.3 lb	1.65 kg
the width of a basketball court	49.21 ft	≈15 meters

1.2 Conversions Between Metric and Imperial Systems, textbook pages 12–18

2. Convert each measure using the indicated units. Round to one decimal place.

   a) 8 kg to pounds

   16 pounds.

   b) 15 qt to fluid ounces

   480 fl oz.

   c) 135°F to degrees Celsius

   135-32=103   103÷$\frac{9}{5}$≈51.22

   d) 3.5 gal to litres to L

   ≈ 13.2 L.

   e) 36 ft to metres

   ≈11 m.

   f) 515 yd to feet

   1545 ft

3. Angie takes medication daily. Her dose is 32 mg per kilogram of body weight. Angie weighs 140 lb. Round your answer to the nearest tenth.

   a) Convert Angie's weight to kilograms.

   ∵ 1 kg = 2lb

   ∴ 140 lb = 70 kg.

   b) How much medication will Angie take in each dose?

   32 × 70 = 2240 mg

4. Some Canadians who live near the Canada-U.S. border fill their gas tanks in the U.S. 边境
   One day, the price of gas is 86.9¢/L in Sarnia and $2.67/gal in Port Huron, Michigan.
   1 U.S. gallon = 3.785 L   萨尼亚 (加拿大)   休伦港 (美国)
   $1.00 U.S. = $1.10 Canadian

   a) What is the price for 1 U.S. gallon in Sarnia?

   86.9 × 3.785 = 328.9165 ¢

   ≈$3.28

   b) Which location offers a better price for gas?

Date: _____

1.3 Similar Triangles, textbook pages 19–29

5. Triangle ABC is similar to triangle DEF. Round your answers to one decimal place.

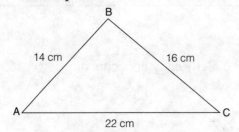

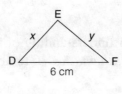

Find the indicated side lengths.

$22 \div 6 \approx 3.67$

$14 \div 3.67 \approx 3.81$ cm = x

$16 \div 3.67 \approx 4.36 = y$

1.4 Solve Problems Using Similar Triangles, textbook pages 30–37

6. To find the height of a building, Rick measured the distance from a flagpole to the building, and from the building to the CN Tower. He then drew a picture of the building, the CN Tower, and the flagpole. Rick drew a straight line from the 360-m mark on the CN Tower to the base of the flagpole. The flagpole is 50 m from the building. The building is 400 m from the CN Tower.

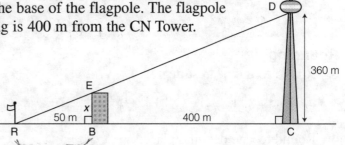

a) How far is the flagpole from the base of the CN Tower?

$400 + 50 = 450$ m

b) Which triangles are similar? How do you know?

$\triangle RBE \sim \triangle RCD$ ∴ $\angle ERB = \angle DRC$, $\angle EBR = \angle DC$

c) How tall is the building?

$\dfrac{450}{50} = 9$ $\dfrac{360}{9} = 40$ $x = 40$

7. Use the measurements taken by a surveyor to find the width of the river to one decimal place.

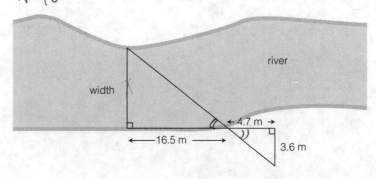

$\dfrac{16.5}{4.7} = 3.5$

$3.6 \times 3.5 = 12.6$

∴ width = 12.6 m.

CHAPTER 2 Right Triangle Trigonometry

Get Set

Answer these questions to check your understanding of the Get Ready concepts on pages 44–45 of the *Foundations of Mathematics 10* textbook.

Solving Proportions

1. Solve each proportion.

   a) $\dfrac{x}{15} = \dfrac{21}{45}$

   $45x = 315$

   $x = 7$

   b) $\dfrac{22}{y} = \dfrac{2}{3}$

   $2y = 66$

   $y = 33$

   c) $\dfrac{18}{23} = \dfrac{z}{46}$

   $23z = 828$

   $z = 36$

   d) $\dfrac{16}{24} = \dfrac{2}{x}$

   $16x = 48$

   $x = 3$

2. Solve each proportion. Express each answer as a decimal. Round your answers to three decimal places.

   a) $\dfrac{x}{11} = \dfrac{4}{14}$

   $14x = 44$

   $x = 3.143$

   b) $\dfrac{18}{y} = \dfrac{8}{30}$

   $8y = 540$

   $y = 67.5$

   c) $\dfrac{x}{3} = \dfrac{19}{8}$

   $8x = 57$

   $x = 7.125$

   d) $\dfrac{15}{t} = \dfrac{6}{13}$

   $6t = 195$

   $t = 32.5$

Rounding

3. Round to the nearest degree.

   a) 14.3° 14°

   b) 11.45° 11°

   c) 31.6° 32°

   d) 82.9° 83°

4. Round to one decimal place.

   a) 22.43 22.4

   b) 163.717 163.7

   c) 2.37 2.4

   d) 0.79 0.8

5. Round to four decimal places.

   a) 0.148 267 315 0.1483

   b) 27.005 19 27.0052

   c) 45.760 315 45.7603

   d) 3.421 832 3.4218

   e) 15.763 21 15.7632

   f) 109.524 719 3 109.5247

2.1 The Pythagorean Theorem

Textbook
pp. 46–53

Warm-Up

1. Square Roots

Calculate the positive square root of each number. Round your answers to one decimal place.

a) 124 $\sqrt{124} \approx 11.1$

b) 68 $\sqrt{68} \approx 8.2$

c) 12 $\sqrt{12} \approx 3.5$

d) 300 $\sqrt{300} \approx 17.3$

2. Types of Triangles

Name this triangle according to its side lengths and angles.

3. Number Sense

Find the value of each variable that makes each statement true.

a) $x^2 = 9^2 + 12^2$

$x = 9 + 12$

$x = 21$

b) $p^2 = 12^2 + 5^2$

$p = 12 + 5$

$p = 17$

4. Math Literacy

Give three examples of places where triangles are used in everyday life.

– clothes hanger

–

5. Types of Triangles

Name this triangle according to its side lengths and angles.

6. Pythagorean Theorem

Choose the correct answers.

The Pythagorean theorem states, in a _____right_____ (left, right, upside down) triangle, the square of the _____legs_____ (triangle, hypotenuse, legs) is equal to the sum of the square of the _____hypotenuse_____ (arms, hypotenuse, legs).

7. Number Sense

Solve for x.

a) $5^2 = x^2 + 4^2$

$x^2 = 5^2 - 4^2$

$x^2 = 25 - 16$

$x = 3$

b) $10^2 = 8^2 + x^2$

$x^2 = 10^2 - 8^2$

$x^2 = 100 - 64$

$x^2 = 36$

$x = 6$

8. Types of Triangles

Name this triangle according to its side lengths and angles.

$I^2 + II^2 = III^2$

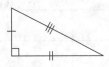

Practise: The Pythagorean Theorem

Section
2.1

1. Calculate the length of each hypotenuse. Round your answer to one decimal place, if necessary.

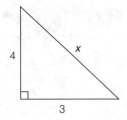
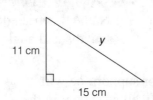
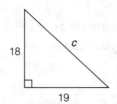
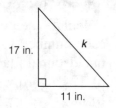

a) ___$x=5$___ b) ___$y=18.6$ cm___ c) ___$c=26.2$___ d) ___$k=20.2$ in___

2. Find the length of the third leg in each triangle. Round your answers to one decimal place.

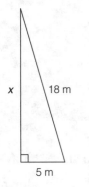
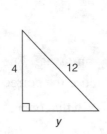
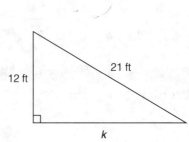
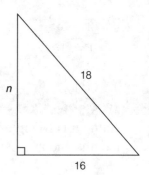

a) ___$x=17.3$ m___ b) ___$y=11.3$___ c) ___$k=17.2$ ft___ d) ___$n=8.2$___

3. To find the length of the third side of the triangle shown on the right, Simone writes $22^2 + 26^2 = x^2$ and plans to solve for x. Is she correct? How do you know?

___No. Because this triangle is not a right triangle.___

_____

_____

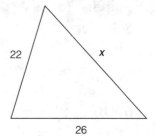

4. Explain to your friend John the steps he will need to follow to solve for x in the triangle shown on the right.

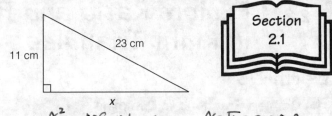

11 cm
23 cm
x

$11^2 + x^2 = 23^2$ ∴ $121 + x^2 = 529$ ∴ $x^2 = 529 - 121 = 408$ $x = \sqrt{408} \approx 20.2$

5. Ricardo is building a shelf in his garage. For support, he will attach three triangle-shaped brackets to the wall as shown in the diagram. Find the length of the third side. Round your answer to one decimal place.

Mar 2J
2022

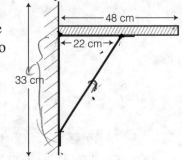

48 cm
22 cm
33 cm
?

$33^2 + 22^2 = 1089 + 484 = 1573$

$\sqrt{1573} \approx 39.7$

6. A 15-ft ladder is placed against a building. The bottom of the ladder is 4 ft out from the wall. You need to find how high up the side of the building the ladder touches the wall.

a) Make a sketch of the situation.

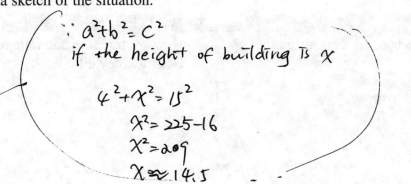

∴ $a^2 + b^2 = c^2$
if the height of building is x

$4^2 + x^2 = 15^2$
$x^2 = 225 - 16$
$x^2 = 209$
$x \approx 14.5$

15
4
building.

b) How far up the side of the building does the top of the ladder reach? Round your answer to one decimal place.

2.2 # Explore Ratio and Proportion in Right Triangles

Textbook
pp. 54–62

Warm-Up

1. Convert Fractions to Decimals	**2. Number Sense**
Write each fraction as a decimal.	Write each fraction in simplest form.
a) $\dfrac{6}{15}$	**a)** $\dfrac{8}{18}$
b) $\dfrac{12}{5}$	**b)** $\dfrac{2}{8}$
c) $\dfrac{7}{8}$	**c)** $\dfrac{3}{24}$
d) $\dfrac{5}{4}$	**d)** $\dfrac{16}{40}$

3. Math Literacy	**4. Ratios**
What is a ratio? Use examples to explain.	Write each ratio in simplest form.
	a) 24:16
	b) 21:28
	c) 8:32
	d) 15:35

5. Mental Math	**6. Math Literacy**
Evaluate without using a calculator.	How are fractions and ratios similar? How are they different?
a) $\sqrt{121}$	
b) $\sqrt{64}$	
c) $\sqrt{100}$	
d) $\sqrt{400}$	

7. Angles in a Triangle	**8. Angles in a Triangle**
Find the value of x.	Find the missing angle measures.

Practise: Explore Ratio and Proportion in Right Triangles

Section 2.2

1. a) In the following right triangle, label the adjacent side relative to ∠D. Draw an arrow from D to show where the opposite side is. Label the opposite side relative to ∠D②

1ar 26

① DE   ② EF

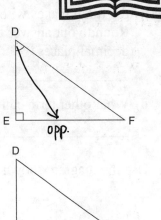

b) What would change if you were asked to label the adjacent and opposite sides relative to ∠F?

opp. DE   Adj. EF

1ar 26 **2.** Find each ratio for the indicated angle. Round your answers to two decimal places.

a) The ratio of the length of the adjacent side relative to ∠M to the length of the hypotenuse relative to ∠M is ____5:7____.

0.71

15:21
↳5.7

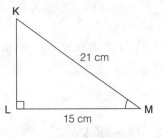

b) The ratio of the length of the adjacent side relative to ∠X to the length of the hypotenuse relative

to ∠X is ___22:41___. $\frac{22}{41}$

0.54

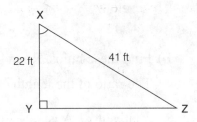

c) The ratio of the length of the adjacent side relative to ∠D to the length of the hypotenuse relative

to ∠D is ___1:2___. $\frac{18.2}{36.4}$

0.9 0.5

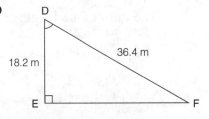

3. A wheelchair ramp reaches 1 m high at its highest point. The length of the ramp is 8.4 m.

a) Label the diagram on the right to represent this situation.

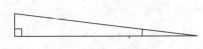

b) Find the length of the third side of the ramp. Round your answer to two decimal places.

c) Find the ratio of the length of the opposite side to the length of the adjacent side relative to the angle the ramp makes with the ground. Round your answer to three decimal places.

> **Hint:** Think of a term you would use to express how steep a roof, a road, or even a ski hill is.

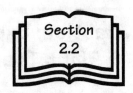
Section 2.2

_____

d) What other term can we use to describe the ratio in part **c)**?

_____

4. Use the diagram shown below to answer the following questions.

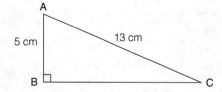

a) Use the Pythagorean theorem to find the length of the third side.

b) Find these ratios. Round your answers to two decimal places.

The ratio of the length of the opposite side relative to $\angle A$ to the length of the hypotenuse

relative to $\angle A$ is _____.

The ratio of the length of the opposite side relative to $\angle C$ to the length of the hypotenuse

relative to $\angle C$ is _____.

2.3 The Sine and Cosine Ratios

Textbook pp. 63–73

Warm-Up

1. Label the Sides	**2. Number Sense**
Label the adjacent side relative to ∠Q and the hypotenuse of this right triangle relative to ∠Q. 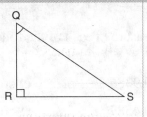	Write a ratio comparing the length of the side opposite ∠F to the length of the hypotenuse. Then, express the ratio as a decimal, rounded to two decimal places. 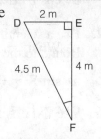
3. Math Literacy	**4. Ratios**
Define an adjacent side.	Write a ratio comparing the length of the side adjacent to ∠M to the length of the hypotenuse. Then, express the ratio as a decimal, rounded to two decimal places. 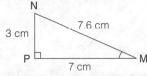
5. Mental Math	**6. Math Literacy**
Without looking at your textbook, name the adjacent side, opposite side and the hypotenuse relative to ∠G. Give one ratio comparing the length of one of two sides to the length of hypotenuse.	Define an opposite side.
7. Comparing Sides	**8. Label the Sides**
Write a ratio comparing the length of the side opposite ∠K to the length of the adjacent side relative to ∠K. Then, express the ratio as a decimal. 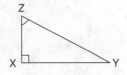	Label the adjacent side and the hypotenuse relative to ∠Z.

Practise: The Sine and Cosine Ratios

Section
2.3

1. Use a scientific calculator to find each value. Round to four decimal places.

   a) cos 75° _____ **b)** sin 12° _____ **c)** sin 53° _____

   d) cos 8° _____ **e)** sin 66° _____ **f)** cos 81° _____

2. Use a scientific calculator to find the angle measure in each of the following.
   Round to the nearest degree.

   a) sin X = 0.1636 _____ **b)** sin A = 0.9386 _____ **c)** cos Y = 0.2232 _____

   d) cos F = 0.5867 _____ **e)** sin B = 0.4587 _____ **f)** cos K = 0.6892 _____

3. In the following right triangles, find the measure of the indicated side.
   Round to the nearest centimetre.

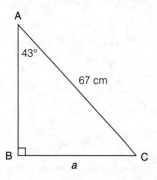

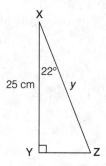

a) $a =$ _____

b) $y =$ _____

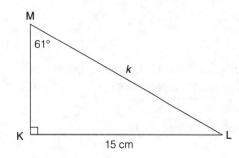

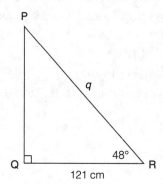

c) $k =$ _____

d) $q =$ _____

4. While mountain climbing, one end of a 22-m-long rope is at the top of a cliff. The angle the rope makes with the ground at the bottom of the cliff is approximately 75°. Approximately how high is the cliff? Round your answer to one decimal place.

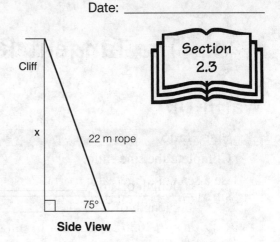

Section 2.3

Side View

5. Mark is looking at sailboats at a boat show. He admires a sailboat with two triangular sails.

a) The side opposite the 35° angle is 16 m. The length of the sail is the hypotenuse. Use the sine ratio to find s. Round your answer to one decimal place.

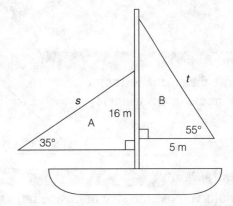

b) The side adjacent to the 55° angle is 5 m. The length of the sail is the hypotenuse. Use the cosine ratio to find t. Round your answer to one decimal place.

2.4 # The Tangent Ratio

Textbook
pp. 74–82

Warm-Up

1. Sine Ratio	**2. Number Sense**

1. Sine Ratio

Complete the sine ratio.

$$\sin x = \frac{\text{length of side } \underline{\hspace{2cm}} x}{\text{length of } \underline{\hspace{2cm}}}$$

2. Number Sense

Find the length of side GH, to the nearest tenth of a centimetre.

$$\sin \underline{\hspace{1cm}}° = \frac{y}{}$$

$$\underline{\hspace{1cm}} \sin \underline{\hspace{1cm}}° = y$$

$$y = \underline{\hspace{2cm}}$$

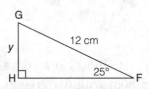

3. Sine Ratio	**4. Cosine Ratio**

3. Sine Ratio

Write the sine ratio for the 42° angle in this triangle.

$$\sin \underline{\hspace{1cm}}° = \frac{m}{}$$

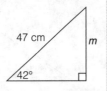

4. Cosine Ratio

Complete the cosine ratio.

$$\cos x = \frac{\text{length of side} \underline{\hspace{2cm}} x}{\text{length of } \underline{\hspace{2cm}}}$$

5. Mental Math	**6. Cosine Ratio**

5. Mental Math

Would you use the sine or cosine ratio to find the length of side *r* of this triangle?

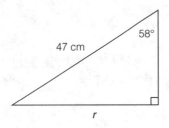

6. Cosine Ratio

Find the length of side LM to the nearest tenth of a centimetre.

$$\cos \underline{\hspace{1cm}}° = \frac{j}{}$$

$$\underline{\hspace{1cm}} \cos \underline{\hspace{1cm}}° = j$$

$$j = \underline{\hspace{2cm}}$$

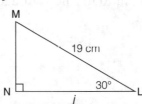

7. Sine or Cosine	**8. Cosine Ratio**

7. Sine or Cosine

Use the sine or cosine ratio to find the length of side *r* for this triangle. Round your answer to one decimal place.

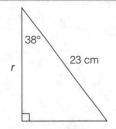

8. Cosine Ratio

Write the cosine ratio for the 32° angle in this triangle.

$$\cos \underline{\hspace{1cm}}° = \frac{p}{}$$

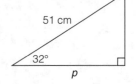

Practise: The Tangent Ratio

Section
2.4

1. Find each value. Round to four decimal places.

   a) tan 22.4° _____   b) tan 75° _____

   c) tan 12° _____   d) tan 45° _____

2. Find each angle measure. Round to the nearest degree.

   a) tan A = 0.6375 _____   b) tan B = 2.6758 _____

   c) tan C = 1.1111 _____   d) tan D = 0.3353 _____

3. Calculate the measure of ∠S to the nearest degree, using a scientific calculator.

   The opposite side relative to ∠S is _____ cm.

   The adjacent side relative to ∠S is _____ cm.

   tan S = ——

   ∠S = _____

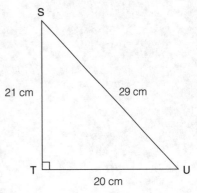

4. Write the tangent ratio for the indicated angle in each triangle shown below. Write your answers as fractions in lowest terms.

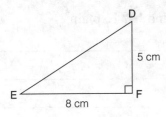
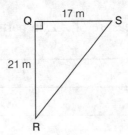
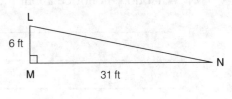

   a) tan D = _____   b) tan R = _____   c) tan N = _____

5. Jeremy uses the Pythagorean theorem and the tangent ratio to solve for ∠B in triangle ABC shown on the right. Explain the error Jeremy made.

   _____

   _____

   _____

   _____

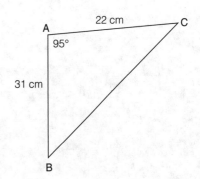

6. To ensure safety, ladders must be placed with a 4:1 ratio. That means, if Keri places his ladder 8 ft up the wall, the base of the ladder must be 2 ft away from the wall.

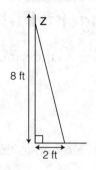

a) Calculate the measure of ∠Z to the nearest degree, using a scientific calculator.

b) Keri extends the ladder and places it 16 ft up the wall. He moves the base to 4 ft away from the wall. Calculate the measure of ∠Z to the nearest degree, using a scientific calculator.

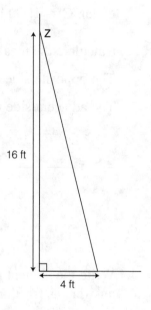

c) What do you notice about the measure of ∠Z in parts **a)** and **b)**? Explain.

_____

_____

_____

_____

2.5 Solve Problems Using Right Triangles

Textbook pp. 83–87

Warm-Up

1. Tangent Ratio

Write the tangent ratio for the 32° angle of this triangle.

$\tan \underline{\quad}° = \dfrac{u}{\underline{\quad}}$

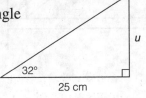

2. Number Sense

Find the length of side e, to the nearest tenth of a centimetre.

$\tan \underline{\quad}° = \dfrac{e}{\underline{\quad}}$

$\underline{\quad} \tan \underline{\quad}° = \underline{\quad}$

$e = \underline{\quad\quad\quad}$

3. Adjacent Sides

What is the length of the side adjacent to the 45° angle labelled in the diagram?

$\underline{\quad}$ cm

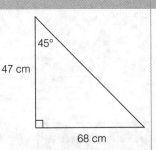

4. Mental Math

Could you use the tangent formula to calculate the length of r? Explain.

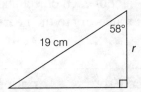

5. Opposite Sides

What is the length of the side opposite the 45° angle labelled in the diagram?

$\underline{\quad}$ m

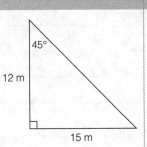

6. Estimation

Pick an object up high in your home and estimate the angle of elevation from where you sit or stand. Write down your estimate. Use your clinometer to check how close you were.

7. Tangent Ratio

Find the length of side e, to the nearest tenth of a centimetre.

$\tan \underline{\quad}° = \dfrac{\underline{\quad}}{d}$

$\underline{\quad} \tan \underline{\quad}° = \underline{\quad}$

$d = \underline{\quad\quad\quad}$

$d = \underline{\quad\quad\quad}$

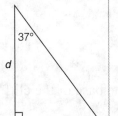

8. Math Literacy

Matthew stands on the balcony of his apartment. He wants to find out the height of the apartment building 50 m away. Would Matthew be measuring the angle of elevation, or the angle of depression, or both?

Practise: Solve Problems Using Right Triangles

Date: _____

1. A large support beam in the frame of a building runs diagonally between two beams, as shown in the diagram.

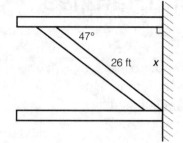

   a) Use the tangent ratio to calculate the length of the side opposite the 47° angle. Round your answer to one decimal place.

   b) Does the support beam form an angle of elevation or an angle of depression with the wall?

2. Raul uses a transit that is 1.2 m above the ground to sight a number of objects. Find the height of each object above the ground. Round your answers to the nearest tenth of a metre.

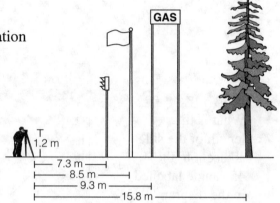

Distance From Object (m)	Angle of Elevation (°)	Height From Transit to Top of Object (m)	Height of Object (m)
8.5	48.2		
9.3	44.2		
15.8	51.3		
7.3	49.6		

3. From the top of a cliff 88 m above the canyon floor, Stefani notes the angle of depression to the edge of the river in the canyon to be 37°.

   a) Sketch and label a model of the situation.

   b) Calculate the horizontal distance from the base of the cliff to the river's edge. Round your answer to the nearest metre.

4. The town bought a new light for the community baseball field. The light is 145 ft above the ground. Justin set the new light on the baseball field at an angle of 50° so it would shine where it was needed.

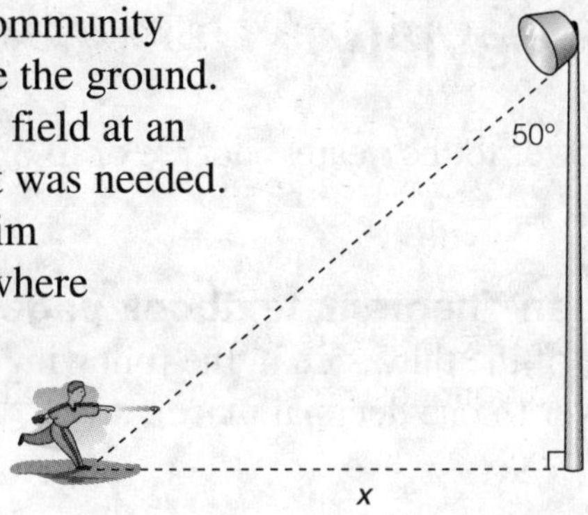

Section 2.5

50°

145 ft

x

   a) Justin's friend Sam came to meet him after work. He waited on the field where the new light was shining. How far is Sam from the light standard? Round your answer to one decimal place.

   b) What is the angle of elevation from Sam to the light fixture?

5. Jeff measures the angle of elevation to the top of a 250 ft high telecommunications tower to be 33° and the angle of depression to the base of the tower to be 16°.

   a) Sketch and label a diagram of the situation.

   b) How far is Jeff from the tower? Round your answer to the nearest foot.

Chapter 2 Review

For all questions, answer to the nearest degree or to one decimal place wherever appropriate.

2.1 The Pythagorean Theorem, textbook pages 46–53

1. Find the measure of the third side in the following triangle. Round your answer to one decimal place.

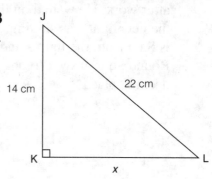

14 cm   22 cm

K   x   L

2.2 Explore Ratio and Proportion in Right Triangles, textbook pages 54–62

2. Label the hypotenuse and the opposite and adjacent sides relative to ∠K in triangle KLM below.

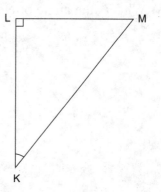

L   M

K

   a) The ratio comparing the length of the opposite side to the length of the adjacent side is _____.

   b) The ratio comparing the length of the adjacent side to the length of the hypotenuse is _____.

   c) The ratio comparing the length of the opposite side to the length of the hypotenuse is _____.

2.3 The Sine and Cosine Ratios, textbook pages 63–73

3. At a ski hill, the chair lift rises 1000 m vertically by travelling along a rail system that is 1600 m long. What angle does the chair lift make with the ground? Round your answer to the nearest tenth of a degree.

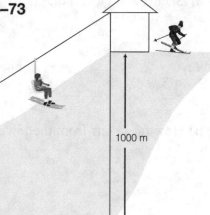

1600 m   1000 m

x

2.4 The Tangent Ratio, textbook pages 74–82

Chapter 2
Review

4. A ramp built inside a stadium for people to move from the main level to the second floor forms an angle of 20° with the main floor. The second floor is 18 ft above the main floor.

   a) Sketch and label a model of the situation.

   b) What is the length of the ramp? Round your answer to the nearest tenth of a foot.

2.5 Solve Problems Using Right Triangles, textbook pages 83–87

5. From the top of a tall building, the base of a second building 50 m away is at an angle of depression of 77°, and the top of the second building is at an angle of elevation of 25°.

   a) Sketch and label a model of the situation.

   b) What is the height of the second building? Round your answer to the nearest tenth of a metre.

CHAPTER 3

Linear Relations

Get Set

Answer these questions to check your understanding of the Get Ready concepts on pages 98–99 of the *Foundations of Mathematics 10* textbook.

Common Factors

1. Find the greatest whole number that divides evenly into each pair of numbers below.

   a) 8 and 12: _____   **b)** 15 and 45: _____   **c)** 11 and 121: _____

Operations With Fractions and Decimals

2. State each fraction in lowest terms.

   a) $\dfrac{4}{8} =$ **b)** $\dfrac{2}{10} =$ **c)** $\dfrac{3}{12} =$ **d)** $\dfrac{21}{35} =$

Operations With Integers

3. Evaluate the following.

   a) $-6 - 7$ **b)** $-14 - (-9)$ **c)** $\dfrac{-7 - (-8)}{12 - (-4)}$

Graphing on a Coordinate Grid

4. Write the coordinates of each point.

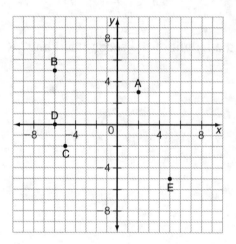

Working With Variables

5. Solve for x.

   a) $2x - 1 = 5$ **b)** $3x - 1 = 8$ **c)** $-x + 7 = 11$

6. Evaluate each expression for $y = -7$.

   a) $\dfrac{y - 5}{3}$ **b)** $\dfrac{y - 4}{-1}$ **c)** $8y - 3$

3.1 Slope as a Rate of Change

Textbook
pp. 100–110

Warm-Up

1. Fractions

Write each fraction in lowest terms.

a) $\dfrac{12}{18}$

b) $\dfrac{14}{35}$

c) $\dfrac{8}{14}$

d) $\dfrac{15}{30}$

2. Number Sense

Find each difference.

a) $3 - (-5)$

b) $-7 - 6$

c) $-2 - (-1)$

d) $6 - 4$

3. Tables of Values

Complete the table of values for $y = 2x + 5$.

x	y
0	
1	
2	
3	
4	

4. Mental Math

Carmindy earns $9/h. What are her total earnings if she works 7 h?

5. Graph a Linear Relation

Create a table of values for $y = 3x + 4$. Then, graph the line.

x	y
−2	
−1	
0	
1	
2	

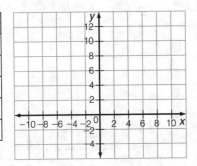

6. Math Literacy

Given the equation of a linear relation, describe how you would make a table of values for the relation.

Practise: Slope as a Rate of Change

1. Use the tables below to create a table of values for each given equation. The *x*-values are provided. Determine the *y*-values and the rate of change in the *y*-values for each equation.

   a) $y = -2x + 2$

x	y	Rate of Change
−2		
−1		
0		
1		
2		

   b) $y = 5x - 1$

x	y	Rate of Change
−2		
−1		
0		
1		
2		

2. Study the table of values below.

x	y	Rate of Change
−1	5	
0	7	
1	9	
2	11	
3	13	

   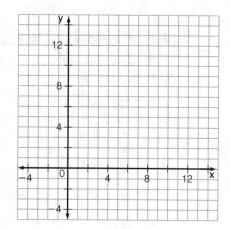

   a) Graph the values from the table on the grid.

   b) Use your table to find the rate of change in the *y*-values.

3. Lewis works at a bookstore in the local mall, where he earns $8.25/h. A typical shift lasts 6 h.

   a) Create a table of values to show his total earnings for up to 6 hours of work.

   b) Determine the rate of change in Lewis's total earnings.

   c) Graph your table of values. Connect the points with a straight line.

Hours Worked	Total Earnings ($)	Rate of Change
0		
1		
2		
3		
4		
5		
6		

   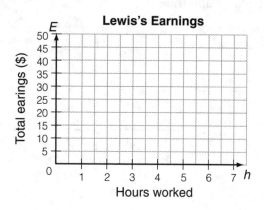

   Lewis's Earnings

d) Choose any two points on the line. Find the rise and run between them.

First point (_____,_____) Second point (_____,_____)

rise: _____ run: _____

e) Find the slope of the line using the rise and run from part **d)**.

slope $= \dfrac{\text{rise}}{\text{run}}$

= _____

= _____

f) The rate of change is _____. This represents _____

_____.

4. The equation of a straight line is $y = 2x + 2$.
   a) Create a table of values for this equation.
   b) Graph your table of values.
      Draw a straight line through the points.
   c) Choose any two points on the line.
      Find the rise and run between them.

   First point (_____,_____)

   Second point (_____,_____)

   rise: _____ run: _____

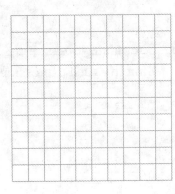

x	y

d) Find the slope of the line.

slope $= \dfrac{\text{rise}}{\text{run}}$

= _____

= _____

5. Amy works on an assembly line packing dolls into boxes to sell in stores. Amy can pack 15 dolls in 1 hour.
   a) Create a table of values to show how many dolls Amy packs in 6 hours of work.
   b) Find the rate of change in the number of dolls Amy packs.
   c) What does the rate of change represent?

   _____

Hours Worked	Number of Dolls Packed	Rate of Change
0		
1		
2		
3		
4		
5		
6		

3.2 Investigate Slope and y-Intercept Using Technology

Textbook pp. 111–117

Warm-Up

1. Math Literacy	2. Number Sense
What is the rate of change of a linear relation? Explain.	Find each difference. **a)** $-10 - 3$ **b)** $-14 - (-6)$ **c)** $8 - (-3)$ **d)** $-1 - (-4)$

3. Simplify Expressions	4. Rate of Change
Simplify each expression. **a)** $\dfrac{5 - 2}{-3 - 6}$ **b)** $\dfrac{-8 - (-4)}{-2 - 10}$	David earns \$6.50/h. Last night he worked 5 h and earned \$32.50. What is the rate of change in David's earnings? _____.

5. Calculate	6. Interpret Slope
The graph shows the total cost for a large pizza with different numbers of toppings. If x represents the number of toppings and y represents the total cost in dollars, find the slope of the line. $m = \dfrac{\text{rise}}{\text{run}}$ $= \underline{\hspace{2cm}}$ $= \underline{\hspace{2cm}}$ $= \underline{\hspace{2cm}}$ 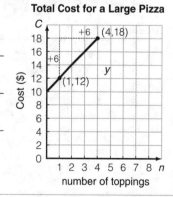	What does the slope of the line in question 5 represent? _____ _____

Practise: Investigate Slope and y-Intercept Using Technology

Section
3.2

1. Graph the following equations using a graphing calculator with the standard window settings. Then, using the graph, calculate the slope and y-intercept of each line.

a) $y = 2x$

slope: _____

y-intercept: _____

b) $y = 4x - 5$

slope: _____

y-intercept: _____

c) $y = -x + 6$

slope: _____

y-intercept: _____

d) $y = -\dfrac{1}{2}x + \dfrac{5}{2}$

slope: _____

y-intercept: _____

Hint: Make sure each equation is stated in the form $y = mx + b$.

2. Write the equation of each line using the information given.

a) slope $= \dfrac{7}{2}$ and y-intercept $= 9$ equation: _____

b) $m = -3$ and $b = 3$ equation: _____

c) $m = 0$ and $b = -3$ equation: _____

d) $m = 7$ and $b = 0$ equation: _____

3. Write the equation for each graph below. First determine the slope and y-intercept.

a)

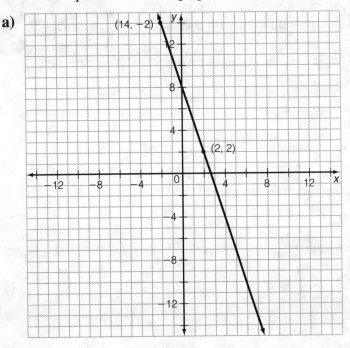

slope: _____

y-intercept: _____

equation: _____

b)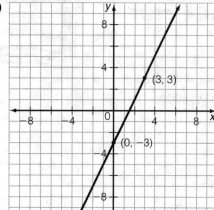

slope: _____

y-intercept: _____

equation: _____

c)

slope: _____

y-intercept: _____

equation: _____

4. The cost to rent a hall for a hockey banquet is modelled by the equation $C = 35n + 3000$, where C represents the total cost in dollars and n represents the number of people attending the banquet.

a) Use a graphing calculator to graph this equation with the standard window settings.

b) Since no line appears on your display screen, describe what you need to do to make the graph appear.

_____

c) What does the number 35 in the equation represent?

_____

d) What does the number 3000 in the equation represent?

_____

e) How much will the banquet cost if the organizers expect 200 people?

_____

3.3 Properties of Slopes of Lines

Textbook
pp. 118–127

Warm-Up

1. Positive Slopes

Determine the slope of the escalator. Express your final answer as a fraction in lowest terms.

$$m = \frac{\text{rise}}{\text{run}}$$

$$= \underline{\hspace{2cm}}$$

$$= \underline{\hspace{2cm}}$$

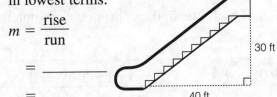

30 ft

40 ft

2. Number Sense

Determine the slope of the ramp for the chicken coop.

$$m = \frac{\text{rise}}{\text{run}}$$

$$= \underline{\hspace{2cm}}$$

2 m

←5 m→

3. Math Literacy

Given the graph of a line, describe how to calculate the slope of the line.

4. Mental Math

Simplify each expression.

a) $\dfrac{12}{-4}$

b) $\dfrac{8}{18}$

c) $\dfrac{-15}{10}$

d) $\dfrac{9}{3}$

5. Slope

Determine the slope of the toboggan run. Write your final answer in lowest terms.

$$m = \frac{\text{rise}}{\text{run}}$$

$$= \underline{\hspace{2cm}}$$

$$= \underline{\hspace{2cm}}$$

30 ft

70 ft

6. Slope

Determine the slope of the ladder. Write your final answer in lowest terms.

$$m = \frac{\text{rise}}{\text{run}}$$

$$= \underline{\hspace{2cm}}$$

$$= \underline{\hspace{2cm}}$$

8 ft

2 ft

Practise: Properties of Slopes of Lines

Section
3.3

1. Consider the following linear equations:

   i) $y = 3x + 4$ **ii)** $y = 4$ **iii)** $y = -\dfrac{1}{2}x + 5$

   iv) $y = x - 2$ **v)** $y = -x - 5$ **vi)** $y = -1$ **vii)** $y = \dfrac{1}{3}x + 5$

   a) On each equation above, circle the slope value.

   b) Based on the slope values, write the equation of each line in the appropriate column in the table below.

Positive Slope	Negative Slope	Zero Slope

2. Write an equation of a line that is

   a) parallel to $y = 4x + 2$ _____

   b) steeper than $y = -x + 7$ _____

   c) less steep than $y = 3x - 1$ _____

   d) parallel to $y = -\dfrac{1}{2}x - 6$ _____

3. Write the equation of the line that is parallel to each line.

   a)

   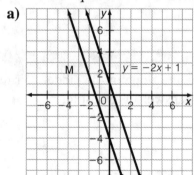

   The equation for line M is

   _____.

   b)

   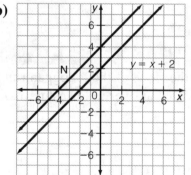

   The equation for line N is

   _____.

Date: _____

c)

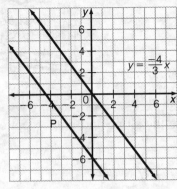

The equation for line P is

_____ .

d)

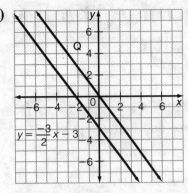

The equation for line Q is

_____ .

4. Maddigan is preparing his dog Pepper for an agility competition. He puts together a dog walk, consisting of two ramps, two bases, and a top plank. Determine the slope of the ramp.

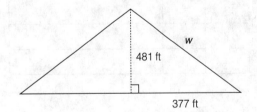

$$s = \frac{\text{rise}}{\text{run}}$$

$$= \underline{\hspace{2cm}}$$

The slope of the ramp is _____ .

5. The Great Pyramid of Egypt was originally approximately 481 ft tall with a base of approximately 754 ft wide. Half of the base is approximately 377 ft. Determine the slope of the side of the Great Pyramid. Express your final answer as a fraction in lowest terms.

$$w = \frac{\text{rise}}{\text{run}}$$

$$= \underline{\hspace{2cm}}$$

$$= \underline{\hspace{2cm}}$$

The slope of the Great Pyramid is _____ .

3.4 Determine the Equation of a Line

Textbook
pp. 128–137

Warm-Up

1. Linear Relations

Determine the slope and *y*-intercept of this line.

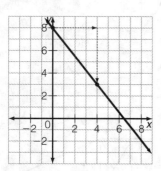

2. Linear Relations

Determine the slope and *y*-intercept of this line.

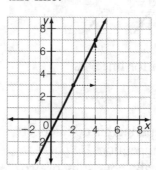

3. Rate of Change

Complete the table of values for the relation $y = -3x + 5$.

x	y	Rate of Change
0		
1		
2		
3		
4		

4. Rate of Change

Complete the table of values for the relation $y = \frac{1}{2}x - 3$.

x	y	Rate of Change
0		
1		
2		
3		
4		

5. y-Intercept

Refer to the table of values. What is the *y*-intercept for this relation?

x	y
−2	−4
−1	0
0	4
1	8
2	12

6. Interpret the Slope

Refer to the relations in questions 3 and 4. Which relation represents a line with a negative slope?

Practise: Determine the Equation of a Line

Section
3.4

1. For each graph below, state **i)** the slope as a fraction in lowest terms,
   ii) the y-intercept, and **iii)** the equation.

a)

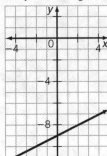

b)

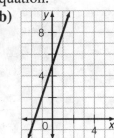

c)

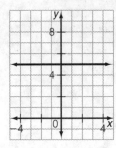

slope: _____   slope: _____   slope: _____

y-intercept: _____ y-intercept: _____ y-intercept: _____

equation: $y =$ _____   equation: $y =$ _____   equation: $y =$ _____

2. Use the given information to write the equation of each line in the form $y = mx + b$.

   a) slope $= -\dfrac{1}{3}$ and y-intercept $= 2$ _____

   b) $m = 4$ and $b = -3$ _____

   c) parallel to $y = 3x - 5$ and y-intercept $= 8$ _____

   d) parallel to $y = 5$ and y-intercept $= -3$ _____

3. Use the given information to write the equation of each line.

   a) slope $= -2$, through the point $(0, 0)$ _____

   b) $m = \dfrac{1}{3}$, through the point $(6, -2)$ _____

   c) $m = -4$, through the point $(4, 8)$ _____

   d) slope $= \dfrac{1}{2}$, through the point $(-4, 5)$ _____

4. Find the equation of the line that passes through this pair of points.

(4, 3) and (2, 9)

Section
3.4

5. Brian takes a beaker and measures its mass. Then, he pours glycerol into the beaker, 50 mL at a time. The masses he measures are given in the table of values below:

Volume of Glycerol (mL)	Mass (g)
0	412
50	525
100	638
150	751
200	864
250	977

a) Use a graphing calculator to graph this data.

b) What is the equation of the line you graphed? _____

c) State the *y*-intercept of the line. Explain what it represents.

_____

d) State the slope of the line. _____

3.5 Graph Linear Relations by Hand

Textbook
pp. 138–145

Warm-Up

1. Evaluate Expressions	**2. Interpret Slope**

1. Evaluate Expressions

Given the relation $y = -x + 3$, find the value of y for each value of x.

a) $x = -4$

b) $x = 1$

2. Interpret Slope

Which of these relations has the steepest slope? How do you know?

a) $y = -2x + 1$

b) $y = -\dfrac{1}{2}x + 3$

c) $y = \dfrac{1}{2}x - 2$

3. Linear Relations	**4. Linear Relations**

3. Linear Relations

Determine if $x = 3$ and $y = -1$ of the point $(3,1)$ satisfy the equation $y = \dfrac{2}{3}x - 1$.

4. Linear Relations

Identify the slope and y-intercept for this relation.

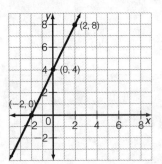

5. Linear Relations	**6. Math Literacy**

5. Linear Relations

Identify the slope and y-intercept for the relation $y = 3x - 1$.

6. Math Literacy

Explain how to determine the slope and y-intercept of the relation $y = 4x - 1$.

Practise: Graph Linear Relations by Hand

1. For each relation, state the slope and *y*-intercept.

a) $y = -\dfrac{1}{4}x + 11$

     slope: _____

     y-intercept: _____

b) $y = 5x - 9$

     slope: _____

     y-intercept: _____

c) $y = \dfrac{4}{5}x$

     slope: _____

     y-intercept: _____

d) $y = -3x + \dfrac{9}{2}$

     slope: _____

     y-intercept: _____

2. Graph each line in question 1.

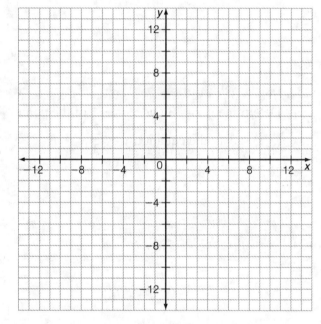

3. Graph each line from the given information.
a) through the points (2, 4) and (6, 9)

b) $m = \dfrac{2}{5}$ and $b = -4$

c) $m = -\dfrac{1}{2}$ and through the point (2, 3)

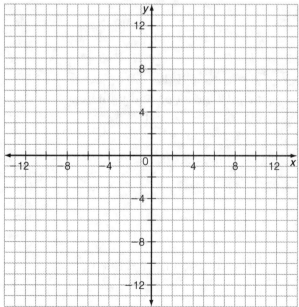

4. A cheetah can run 33 m in one second.

a) Use this information to create a table of values starting at $t = 0$ and going to $t = 4$ s.

Time (s)	0	1	2	3	4
Distance (m)					

b) Plot the data in the table and draw a line passing through the points.

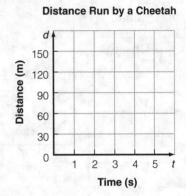

Distance Run by a Cheetah

c) Find the equation of the line you drew in part **b)**. _____

5. Jennie plans to enter a walkathon at school, to raise money for a children's charity. Her neighbour sponsored her for $15.00 per kilometre.

a) Create a table of values for the 4-km walkathon.

Distance (km)	0	1	2	3	4
Funds Raised ($)					

b) Plot the points, then join them with a line.

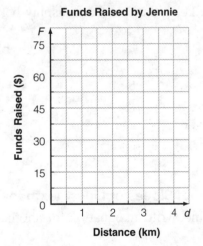

Funds Raised by Jennie

c) Find the equation for the line.

The equation for the line is _____.

Chapter 3 Review

3.1 Slope as a Rate of Change, textbook pages 100-110

1. **a)** The following table of values contains coordinates from points on a straight line. Determine the rate of change in the *y*-values and fill in the missing *x*- and *y*-values.

   Hint: Begin by filling in the second and third empty rate of change boxes. What values must be entered in the other rate of change boxes?

   b) Graph the data in the table.

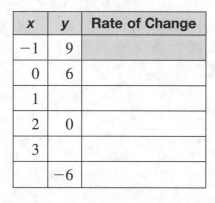

x	y	Rate of Change
−1	9	
0	6	
1		
2	0	
3		
	−6	

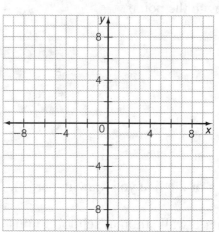

   c) What is the slope of the line? _____

3.2 Investigate Slope and *y*-Intercept Using Technology, textbook pages 111–117

2. Set the **TBLSET** function on a graphing calculator to start at 0 and go up in increments of 1. Use the **G-T** function and the standard window settings to graph the following linear relations. Sketch the calculator display below.

   a) $y = x$

   b) $y = -\frac{1}{3}x + 2$

3.3 Properties of Slopes of Lines, textbook pages 118–127

3. For each line, write an equation for another line parallel to it.

   a) $y = 6x - 5$ _____

   b) $y = -2x + 3$ _____

   c) $y = \frac{1}{2}x + 6$ _____

Date: _____

3.4 Determine the Equation of a Line, textbook pages 128–137

4. Determine the equation of each line given the following information.

a) $m = 3$, y-intercept $= -1$ _____

b) slope $= -2$, $b = 3$ _____

c) $m = 0$, $b = 4$ _____

d) slope $= 2.5$, y-intercept $= -1$ _____

5. Determine the equation of each line.

a) $m = -6$, passing through the point $(1, 7)$ _____

b) $m = \dfrac{1}{2}$, passing through the point $(2, 9)$ _____

c) $m = -\dfrac{1}{3}$, passing through the origin _____

d) $m = \dfrac{5}{8}$, passing through the point $(16, 6)$ _____

3.5 Graph Linear Relations by Hand, textbook pages 138–145

6. Jordan owns a mint-condition rookie card of a famous hockey player. Four years ago, he bought it for $23. Since then, the card has grown in value by $12 each year.

a) Create a table of values to show the card's growth in value over the past 4 years.

Year					
Value of Card ($)					

b) Graph the data from your table of values in part a).

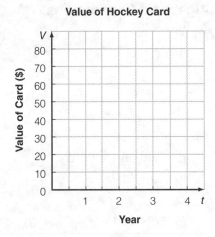

Value of Hockey Card

c) Write the equation that models the card's growth in value. _____

d) What is the card's value at the end of 4 years? _____

CHAPTER 4 Linear Equations

Get Set

Answer these questions to check your understanding of the Get Ready concepts on pages 152–153 of the *Foundations of Mathematics 10* textbook.

Fractions

1. Find the least common multiple of the numbers in each set.
   a) 15 and 12   **b)** 4 and 3   **c)** 8 and 16   **d)** 10 and 11

2. Simplify. Write your answers as fractions in lowest terms.
   a) $\dfrac{1}{3} + \dfrac{1}{4}$ **b)** $\dfrac{4}{5} - \dfrac{3}{4}$ **c)** $\dfrac{2}{5} \times \dfrac{1}{2}$ **d)** $\dfrac{2}{5} \div \dfrac{3}{4}$

Integers

3. Simplify.
   a) $1 + 2 - (-3) + (-4)$ **b)** $3 + (-2)(-4) - (-3) - 6$

   c) $-2(6) + 5 - 1 - (-3)(2) + 4$ **d)** $-2 + 5 - (-6) + 1$

Algebraic Expressions

4. Simplify.
   a) $3x + 2x - x$ **b)** $4x - 2y + 3x - 6y$

   c) $x + y - 2 - (-2x + 6y - 5)$ **d)** $-(k + 6) - (2 - k) + (8 + 4k)$

5. Expand and simplify.
   a) $4(2y - 3)$ **b)** $2(x + y) - 4(x - 3y)$

   c) $2(3x + 1) - 5(2x - 6)$ **d)** $-3(2y - 2) + 4(2y - 1)$

6. Evaluate each expression in question 5 for $x = -1$ and $y = 3$.

4.1 Solve One- and Two-Step Linear Equations

Textbook
pp. 154–162

Warm-Up

1. Add Fractions Simplify. $\dfrac{2}{3} + \dfrac{4}{5}$	**2. Algebra** Simplify. $4x + 2x - 5x$
3. Integers Simplify. $6 - (-2) + (-4) - 3 + 2 - (-1)$	**4. Math Literacy** Your friend missed the class on how to find the slope between two points. Explain to your friend how to find the slope between points (5, 7) and (11, 19).
5. Slope Calculate the slope of the line that passes through (2, 7) and (5, 1)	**6. Solve One-Step Equations** Solve for x. $4x = 32$
7. Solve Equations With Fractions Solve for x. $\dfrac{5x}{8} = 10$	**8. Solve Two-Step Equations** Solve for x. $3x - 7 = 8$

Practise: Solve One- and Two-Step Linear Equations

Section
4.1

1. Use a flow chart to describe the steps needed to solve each equation. Solve each equation.

   a) $3x = -21$

   b) $2x + 3 = 7$

   c) $x - 3 = 8$

   d) $\dfrac{x}{3} = 4$

2. Solve each linear equation.

   a) $x + 1 = 6$

   b) $2t = 8$

   c) $y - 2 = 6$

   d) $\dfrac{k}{4} = 2$

3. Check your solutions in question 2 by using a different method to solve each linear equation. For example, you might use algebra tiles, a flow chart, or opposite operations.

4. Solve.

   a) $\dfrac{k}{3} - 2 = 1$

   b) $\dfrac{3t}{5} = 9$

   c) $\dfrac{y}{3} - 2 = 4$

   d) $\dfrac{-2x}{5} = 4$

5. Check your solutions in question 4 by using a different method to solve each linear equation.

6. Use a flow chart to solve each linear equation.

a) $2x + 4 = 12$

b) $8 = 5x - 2$

c) $\dfrac{x}{2} + 1 = 5$

d) $\dfrac{x}{5} - 1 = 4$

e) $-3x + 1 = 8$

f) $\dfrac{(x - 4)}{2} = 9$

7. Check that $x = 3$ is the solution to the equation $4x - 7 = 5$.

8. The area of a trapezoid is given by the formula.

$$A = \left(\dfrac{a + b}{2}\right)h$$

a) Find the area of a trapezoid if $a = 4$ cm, $b = 12$ cm, and $h = 9$ cm.

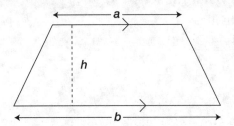

b) The area of a trapezoid is 840 in². If $a = 15$ in. and $b = 20$ in., find h.

9. Yvette is the owner of a dance studio. Through fundraising, her dancers raised $4410 to buy costumes for the upcoming dance recital. Each costume costs $125.

a) Write an equation showing the relationship between the total cost C, in dollars, of the costumes and the number n, of costumes needed.

b) If there are 42 dancers, what will be the total cost of their costumes?

c) Did the dancers raise enough money?

d) If they raised enough money, find how much will be left over. If they did not raise enough, find how much more money is needed.

Date: _____

4.2 Solve Multi-Step Linear Equations

Textbook
pp. 163–173

Warm-Up

1. Multiply Fractions	**2. Algebra**
Multiply. Write your answers in lowest terms. $\dfrac{3}{4} \times \dfrac{2}{5}$	Find the value of m if $x = 2$, $y = 5$, and $b = 1$. $y = mx + b$
3. Divide Fractions	**4. Math Literacy**
Divide. $\dfrac{4}{9} \div \dfrac{2}{3}$	Use examples to explain "variable term" and "constant term" to a new student in your class.
5. Integers	**6. Algebra Tiles**
Simplify. $5 - (-2) + 12 \div (-2)$	Use algebra tiles to model the equation $3x + 4 = 4x - 2$. Sketch the tiles.
7. Solve Multi-Step Equations	**8. Solve Equations With Brackets**
Solve the equation $5x - 7 = 3x - 1$.	Solve the equation $2(x - 1) + 4 = -(x + 6) + 5$.

Practise: Solve Multi-Step Linear Equations

Section
4.2

1. List, in order, the steps to solve each equation.

a) $\dfrac{(6x - 2)}{5} = 2$

b) $\dfrac{2}{5}(k + 1) = 2$

c) $16 = 4(2a - 1)$

d) $\dfrac{22t + 1}{3} = 15$

2. Solve each equation in question 1.

3. Solve each equation by modelling with algebra tiles.

a) $4d = 5d - 8$

b) $2x - 5 = 3x + 2$

c) $5t + 1 = 2t - 8$

d) $7p - 3 = 2p + 2$

4. Sandeep and Erin are asked to solve the equation $x + 2 = 2x - 1$.
   Sandeep's first step is $x - 2x = -1 - 2$.
   Erin's first step is $2 + 1 = 2x - x$.
   Who is correct? Explain.

5. Solve each equation.

a) $\dfrac{(6k + 2)}{4} = 5$

b) $2(x + 5) = 3(x - 1)$

c) $\dfrac{3y}{5} - \dfrac{2y}{3} = 4$

d) $\dfrac{(2t + 1)}{3} = 1$

6. Solve each equation.

   a) $0.4x + 5 = 7.8$ **b)** $0.6k = 5 - 0.4k$

> **Hint:** you may find both equations easier to solve if you multiply both sides of each equation by 10.

7. In $\triangle ABC$, the measure of $\angle B$ is twice that of $\angle A$. The measure of $\angle C$ is three times that of $\angle A$.

   a) Find the measures of all three angles.

   b) State the type of triangle this is.

8. Jenni and 11 friends decide to go skydiving. Jenni contacts two companies to get prices. On the Edge Sky Diving Services, charges a group fee of $200 plus $130 per person. JerrMo, charges $145 per person and no group fee.

   a) Write an equation to model the total cost for each company. Use the form $y = mx + b$.

   b) Which company offers the better deal for the 12 skydivers?

9. Randy borrows $400 from his parents to buy a new snowboard. He plans to pay them a fixed amount each week. The amount still owing is modelled by the equation $A = 400 - 50n$, where n represents the number of weeks since Randy borrowed the money.

   a) How many weeks will it take Randy to pay off the loan?

> **Hint:** at that point what will A equal?

   b) How much will Randy owe after 5 weeks?

   c) At the 5-week mark, how much longer will it take Randy to pay off the loan?

4.3 Model With Formulas

Textbook
pp. 174–183

Warm-Up

1. Fractions	2. Solve One-Step Equations
Simplify. $\dfrac{1}{9} + \dfrac{2}{3} \times \dfrac{3}{4}$	Solve. $2x = 28$

3. Solve Multi-Step Equations	4. Math Literacy
Solve. $6(x - 5) = -4x$	Venetia missed the class on solving multi-step equations. Explain to Venetia how to solve $3x - 1 = 20$.

5. Evaluate an Expression	6. Distance, Speed, and Time
Given $P = 2(l + w)$, find l if $P = 36$ cm and $w = 4$ cm.	It took Christine 3 h to travel 177 km. What was her average speed?

7. Simple Interest	8. Rearrange a Formula
Dave's bank account pays simple interest of 1.25% each year. How long will it take to earn \$60 interest on a deposit of \$800?	The formula for the surface area of a square-based prism is $SA = 2l^2 + 4lh$. Rearrange this formula to isolate h.

Practise: Model with Formulas

1. Rearrange each formula to isolate the indicated variable.

   a) $I = Prt$ for t

   b) $PV = nRT$ for V

   c) $d = vt + \dfrac{1}{2}at^2$ for a

   d) $y = mx + b$ for m

2. **a)** Rearrange the formula $A = \dfrac{1}{2}(a + b)h$ to isolate b.

   b) Use the rearranged formula to find b if $A = 28$ cm², $a = 6$ cm, and $h = 8$ cm.

   c) To find b, substitute the values from part **b)** into the original formula (without rearranging first).

   d) Which method should Tarrik use if he finds it difficult to manipulate formulas? Explain.

   e) Which method should Keisha use if she must solve several similar problems? Explain.

3. **a)** Rearrange the formula $d = vt$ to isolate v.

   b) Rearrange the formula $d = vt$ to isolate t.

   c) Use your rearranged formulas to fill in the table.

distance (m)	time (s)	velocity (m/s)
4	3	
6		2
	5	15
28		4
	11	11
85	5	

4. The Starlight Salon offers birthday party packages. There is a flat fee of $200 plus a charge for each treatment. A facial costs $11, a manicure is $18, and a pedicure is $14.

a) Model the cost of a salon party using C for total cost, f for the number of facials done, m for manicures, and p for pedicures.

b) During a party, Starlight's staff did 11 facials, 15 manicures, and 8 pedicures. Use your equation from part a) to find the total cost of the party.

5. The formula $K = 1.6M$ can be used to convert distance in miles (M) to distance in kilometres (K). Use a calculator to answer the questions below.

a) Use the given formula to find out how many kilometres there are in

i) 38 mi   ii) 225 mi   iii) 1000 mi

b) Rearrange the formula to isolate M.

c) Use the formula from part b) to find the number of miles in

i) 25 km

ii) 453 km

iii) 100 km

d) Use one of the formulas above to convert 55 mph to kilometres per hour.

6. A train travels 225 km in 3 h.

a) Find the train's speed in kilometres per hour.

b) How long would it take to travel 550 km at the same speed?

7. Monica made $500 in simple interest on an investment of $4000 over 2 years. Use the formula $I = Prt$ to find the rate of interest she was paid.

4.4 Convert Linear Equations From Standard Form

Textbook pp. 184–189

Warm-Up

1. Integers	2. Solve an Equation
Simplify. $3(4)(5) - (6)(2)(3)$	Solve. $\dfrac{x}{4} - 5 = 0$

3. Solve a Multi-Step Equation	4. Math Literacy
$\dfrac{6x + 5}{5} = 7$	Complete the following words. **a)** The s _ _ _ _ is a measure of the steepness of a line. **b)** The equation $5x + 3y + 8 = 0$ is written in s _ _ _ _ _ _ _ _ _ _ _ _.

5. Isolate y	6. Write an Equation in Slope y-Intercept Form
Rearrange $4x + y - 1 = 6$ to isolate y.	Write the equation $6x - 2y + 8 = 0$ in slope y-intercept form.

7. Identify the Slope and y-Intercept	8. Find the Slope and y-Intercept
Identify the slope and y-intercept of the line.	Find the slope and y-intercept of the line defined by the equation $x - 3y - 12 = 0$.

For question 7 graph:

$3x - 4y - 8 = 0$

Practise: Convert Linear Equations From Standard Form

Section
4.4

1. The linear equations are written in standard form. List the steps needed to rearrange each equation into slope y-intercept form.

   a) $x + y - 3 = 0$

   b) $-12x - 4y - 8 = 0$

   c) $-3x + 5y - 15 = 0$

   d) $8x - 2y + 11 = 0$

2. Write each equation in slope y-intercept form. Then, state its slope and y-intercept.

   a) $3x + y - 5 = 0$

   b) $-x + y = 0$

   c) $y - 4 = 0$

   d) $-2x + 5y - 15 = 0$

3. Verify your answers in question 2 using a CAS.

4. The line $2x + 5y + C = 0$ goes through the point $(1, 7)$. Find the value of C.

5. The line $Ax - 2y + 4 = 0$ goes through the point $(1, 3)$. Find the value of A.

Section
4.4

6. The line $y = mx - 7$ goes through the point $(3, 5)$. Find the value of m.

7. Wembley banquet hall charges a flat fee of $2000 for a rental, and a per-person fee of $42.
   a) Write a linear equation to model the total cost in dollars (C) of holding a banquet for n people.

   b) How much did it cost to hold a banquet for 250 people?

8. Chisholm banquet hall charges a flat fee of $2500 and a per-person fee of $44.
   a) Write a linear equation to model the cost in dollars (C) of holding a banquet for n people.

   b) How much will it cost to hold a banquet for 250 people?

   c) How does the total cost of a banquet for 250 people at Chisholm Hall compare to the total cost of a banquet for 250 people at Wembley Hall?

Chapter 4 Review

Chapter 4
Review

4.1 Solve One- and Two-Step Linear Equations, textbook pages 154–162

2. Solve each linear equation.

a) $x - 11 = 8$

b) $2t = 14$

c) $h + 5 = 9$

d) $\dfrac{b}{(-2)} = -3$

3. Solve.

a) $3x - 1 = 14$

b) $\dfrac{t}{3} - 4 = 0$

c) $6 = 4 - 2k$

d) $6 = \dfrac{(x - 2)}{3}$

4.2 Solve Multi-Step Linear Equations, textbook pages 163–172

4. Solve each equation.

a) $2t + 3 = -t + 12$

b) $\dfrac{2}{3}(x + 2) = 6$

c) $\dfrac{(x + 6)}{4} = 5$

d) $2(y - 5) = 5(y - 8)$

> **Hint:** you could multiply both sides by 10 to make solving parts a) and b) easier.

e) $0.6(2x + 2) = -0.1(2x + 5)$

f) $6.4(2k + 3) = 19.2$

4.3 Model With Formulas, textbook pages 174–183

5. a) Rearrange the formula $I = Prt$ to isolate P.

Chapter 4
Review

b) Rearrange the formula $I = Prt$ to isolate r.

c) Rearrange the formula $I = Prt$ to isolate t.

6. Use the rearranged formulas from question 5 to complete the table.

Hint: Before using a percent in a formula, convert it to a decimal.

Interest ($)	Principal ($)	rate (%)	time (years)
500	2000		4
	600	5.5%	2
120	1200	4%	
450		5%	9

4.4 Convert Linear Equations From Standard Form, textbook pages 184–189

7. Rearrange each equation from standard form to slope y-intercept form.
State the slope and y-intercept.
a) $x + 4y - 16 = 0$ **b)** $3x - 2y + 10 = 0$

c) $8x + 5y - 15 = 0$ **d)** $3x + y = 0$

8. Find the value for b if the line represented by the equation $y = 4x + b$ passes through each point.
a) $(0, -5)$ **b)** $(6, 2)$

c) $(9, 5)$ **d)** $(-4, -1)$

CHAPTER 5 Linear Systems

Get Set

Answer these questions to check your understanding of the Get Ready concepts on pages 196–197 of the *Foundations of Mathematics 10* textbook.

Algebraic Expressions

1. Collect like terms to simplify each expression.

   a) $6c + 4 + 1 - 4c$
   b) $-5x + 3 + 2x - 12$
   c) $3x - 5y + 11 + 4y - 3x - 1$

Manipulate and Solve Equations

2. Rearrange each equation to isolate x.

   a) $3x - 9y = 21$
   b) $5x - 15y - 20 = 0$
   c) $3x + 4y = 18$
   d) $4y = 2x + 5$

3. Solve each equation for x when $y = 3$.

   a) $x = y + 11$
   b) $y = 5x - 2$
   c) $2x + 3y = 15$

Graph Linear Relations

4. Graph the following linear relation. State the slope and y-intercept.

   $y = 3x - 4$

   slope: _____

   y-intercept: _____

Translate Words to Algebra

5. Write an algebraic equation that models each situation. Define all variables used.

   a) The sum of Leah's age and Joan's age is 29.

   b) The total cost of renting a piece of equipment includes a flat fee of $25 and an hourly fee of $10/h.

5.1 # Solve Linear Systems by Graphing

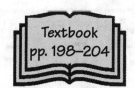 Textbook pp. 198–204

Warm-Up

1. Number Operations	2. Algebra
Evaluate.	Rearrange each equation to isolate y.

1. Number Operations

Evaluate.

a) $\dfrac{2}{3}(3) + \dfrac{1}{2}$

b) $\dfrac{2(-5) + 3(2)}{2}$

c) Rewrite part **b)** as the sum of two fractions each having 2 as its denominator.

2. Algebra

Rearrange each equation to isolate y.

a) $2x + y = 7$

b) $6x + 3y + 12 = 0$

3. Linear Relations

a) Draw an example of a graph that represents a linear relation.

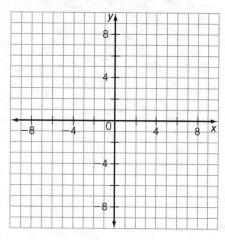

b) What would the point $(0, 1)$ represent on the graph of a linear equation?

4. Algebraic Expressions

Evaluate each expression for the given value of x.

a) $y = 3x - 7$ $x = 4$

b) $2x - y = 4$ $x = -1$

c) $y = -\dfrac{1}{3}x + 5$ $x = 6$

5. Estimation

If an object is moving at a constant rate of 2.2 m/s, approximately how far will it travel in 1 min?

6. Math Literacy

Rearrange the linear equation $-2x + y = 5$ into slope y-intercept form.

Practise: Solve Linear Systems by Graphing

Section
5.1

1. Provide an example of each of the following.
   a) a linear equation **b)** a linear system **c)** the point of
   intersection
   of two lines

   _____   _____   _____

2. **a)** Rearrange the following equations into slope
   y-intercept form.

   $-2x = -y + 1$ ① _____

   The slope is _____ and the y-intercept is _____.

   $x = -y + 4$ ② _____

   The slope is _____ and the y-intercept is _____.

   b) Use the slope and y-intercept to graph each line
   on the same coordinate grid. Label each line with
   its equation.

   c) What is the point of intersection of the two lines?

   (____, ____)

   d) Check these coordinates in each of the original equations.
   Equation ①

   LS =   RS =

   Equation ②

   LS =   RS =

   e) What is the solution to this linear system? (____, ____).

3. Consider the linear system $y = 20x + 150$ and $y = 30x + 100$.
   a) Use a graphing calculator to graph both equations in the same window. Choose an
   appropriate viewing window.

   b) What is the point of intersection of the two linear equations? (____, ____)

4. Solve this linear system by graphing. You can use either the grid provided or a graphing calculator

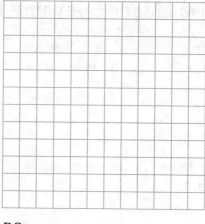

Section 5.1

a) $y = 3x + 4$ ① and $y = 2x + 6$ ②

b) The point of intersection is

(——, ——)

c) Check these coordinates in each of the equations.

Equation ①

LS =   RS =

Equation ②

LS =   RS =

5. Riverside Golf and Country Club runs a women's league in the summer. The cost to join is $300 plus $25 per round of golf played. South Shore Golf Course also offers a women's league. Their membership fee is $400, but they charge only $20 per round played.

a) Write an equation to model the cost to join the women's league at Riverside. Let y represent the total cost and x represent the number of rounds played.

$y =$ ___ $x +$ ___

b) Write an equation to model the cost to join the women's league at South Shore. Let y represent the total cost and x represent the number of rounds played.

$y =$ ___ $x +$ ___

c) Use a graphing calculator to find the point of intersection of the two equations. What does this point represent in terms of the cost of each membership?

The point of intersection is (——, ——).

This means that _____

_____

5.2 Solve Linear Systems by Substitution

Textbook
pp. 205–211

Warm-Up

1. Number Operations	**2. Algebra**
Evaluate. **a)** $3(4) + 12 - 4(2 + 4)$ **b)** $(1 + 2 + 3) - (4 + 5 + 6)$	Identify which variable would be easier to solve for. Explain why. **a)** $3x + y = 11$ **b)** $x - 2y + 14 = 0$
3. Linear Relations	**4. Math Literacy**
Consider the line defined by the equation $2x + y = 4$. **a)** Rewrite the equation in the slope y-intercept form. **b)** What is the slope? **c)** What is the y-intercept?	Describe two ways to graph the line represented by the equation $y = \dfrac{1}{4}x - 3$.
5. Estimation	**6. Tables of Values**
If Celia earns \$8.95/h at her job, about how much does she make in 8.5 h?	Complete the table of values for the relation $y = -x + 5$. | x	y
−2	
−1	
0	
1	
2		

Practise: Solve Linear Systems by Substitution

Section
5.2

1. Why is the substitution method for solving a linear system given that name?

_____

_____

2. Solve the following linear system by substitution.
$y = 2x + 1$ ① $y = 3x - 13$ ②

a) Substitute the expression for y from ① into the other equation.

② _____ $= 3x - 13$

b) Solve for x by arranging the variable terms on one side of the equation and the constant terms on the other side.

_____ $=$ _____

__ $x =$ ____

$x =$ ____

c) Substitute the value for x into one of the original equations and solve for y.
Using $y = 2x + 1$,

$y = 2($ ____ $) + 1$

$y =$ ____ $+ 1$

$y =$ ____

d) Check your answer by substituting the x- and y-values that you determined in parts c) and d) into the other equation.

For $y = 3x - 13$,

LS =   RS =

Is the left side equal to the right side? _____

The solution to this linear system is (____, ____).

3. Solve each linear system by substitution.
a) $y = x + 3$ and $2x + 4y = 4$ b) $y = x - 5$ and $3x - 5y = 9$

4. Dianne is looking for a banquet hall for her school's winter semi-formal dance. The first hall she calls charges $1000 plus $14 per person, while a second hall charges $800 plus $16 per person. She needs to compare the costs of the two halls to decide which offers a better deal for the school dance.

Section
5.2

a) Write linear equations to model the total cost of each hall. Let *y* represent the total cost for each hall and *x* represent the number of people attending the dance.

First hall: $y = \underline{\hspace{1cm}} x + \underline{\hspace{1cm}}$

Second hall: $y = \underline{\hspace{1cm}} x + \underline{\hspace{1cm}}$

b) Solve the system of linear equations using substitution.

i) Substitute the expression for *y* from one equation into the other equation. Solve for *x*.

ii) Substitute the value of *x* determined in part **i)** into one of the equations and solve for *y*.

iii) Check your answer by substituting *x* and *y* into the other equation.

iv) Therefore, the solution is (___, ___).

c) What does the solution in part **b)** represent?

d) If Dianne's school anticipates that 150 people will attend the dance, which hall should they choose?

5.3 Solve Linear Systems by Elimination

Textbook
pp. 212–218

Warm-Up

1. Number Operations	2. Algebra
Evaluate. **a)** $4(3) + 2(6) - 12$ **b)** $(2 \times 3 \times 1) + (2 \times 5) - (3 \times -2)$	Simplify. **a)** $7x + 12x - 2 + 24$ **b)** $-2y + 6x + 2y + 34$

3. Linear Systems	4. Math Literacy
Is the point $(0, 2)$ the solution to the linear system $y = 2x - 4$ and $y = -x + 2$? Explain.	What is considered to be the break-even point for a business product?

5. Estimation	6. Manipulate Linear Equations
Estimate the amount of GST that would be added to each price. GST is 6%. **a)** $150.00 **b)** $19.99	Rearrange the equation to isolate x. $5x - 3y = 10$

Practise: Solve Linear Systems by Elimination

1. Why is the elimination method for solving linear systems given that name?

_____

_____

2. Solve the following linear system by elimination.

$2x + y = 8$ ① $-2x + 3y = 0$ ②

a) Add or subtract the equations to eliminate one variable.

b) Solve the equation in part a) for the remaining variable.

c) Substitute the value determined for the variable in part b) into equation ① and solve for the other variable.

d) Check your answer by placing the values for x and y into equation ②.

The solution to this linear system is (___, ___).

3. Solve the following linear system by elimination.

$8x - 11y = 5$ ① $4x + 17y = 25$ ②

Hint: Adding or subtracting these equations will not eliminate a variable for this linear system.

Section
5.3

a) Multiply equation ② by _____ to eliminate the variable _____ when the equations are _____.

The new equation ③ is _____.

b) Add or subtract equations ① and ③ to eliminate the variable.

c) Solve the equation in part **a)** for the remaining variable.

d) Substitute the value determined in part **c)** into equation ① and solve for the other variable.

e) Check your answer by placing the values for x and y into equation ②.

The solution to this linear system is (____, ____).

4. Describe what you would do with the following linear systems to eliminate one variable.

a) $2x + y = 2$ ① $3x - 2y = 10$ ②

_____

_____

b) $3x - y = 14$ ① $2x - y = 10$ ②

_____

_____

5.4 Solve Problems Involving Linear Systems

Textbook
pp. 219–227

Warm-Up

1. Number Operations

Evaluate.

a) $2(6 + 2) + 4(3) - 7$

b) $\dfrac{(6 + 2)}{4 - 2(-3)}$

2. Algebra

Add the equations in each pair.

a)
$$-2x + y = 12$$
$$+2x + 3y = 2$$

b)
$$4x + 3y = 22$$
$$+x - 3y = 7$$

3. Linear Relations

Do the data in the table below represent a linear relation? Explain your answer.

Time (s)	Distance (m)
10	1.0
15	1.5
20	2.5
30	4.0

4. Math Literacy

Throughout this chapter you have been asked to solve given linear systems. Describe what that means, regardless of the method used to determine the solution.

5. Estimation

In 2006, a company experienced a 5.1% drop in profits compared to their $125 000 profit in 2005. Estimate this company's profits in 2006.

6. Linear Systems

Solve this linear system.
$$y = 3x + 4$$
$$y = -2x + 9$$

Practise: Solve Problems Involving Linear Systems

1. Rearrange the linear system $2x + y = -3$ ① and $3x - y = 8$ ② to isolate y for each equation.
   Solve by graphing with a graphing calculator.

   The solution is (____, ____).

2. Solve the linear system in question 1 using the elimination method.
   a) Add or subtract the equations to eliminate a variable.

   b) Solve the equation in part **a)** for the remaining variable.

   c) Substitute the value determined in part **b)** into equation ① and solve for the other variable.

   d) Check your answer by placing the values for x and y into the original equation ②.

   The solution to this linear equation is (____, ____).

For questions 3 to 5, use your preferred method for solving linear systems.

Section
5.4

3. Jordan's hockey team earns 2 points for a win and 1 point for a tie. They receive no points for a loss. Last season the team played 28 games and lost 9 of them. They had a total of 34 points. Let x represent the number of wins and y represent the number of ties.

   a) Write an equation to represent the total number of games won and tied.

   b) Write an equation to represent the total number of points earned by Jordan's team.

   c) Solve this linear system to find the number of games won and the number of games tied.

   d) Which method for solving linear systems did you use for part c)? Why?

4. Tony has started a lawn-mowing business for the summer. He charges customers a flat fee of $50 to sign up and $5 per week. He knows that his biggest competition is his neighbour Mike, who charges $10 per week and no flat fee.

   a) Write the linear equations that represent Tony's and Mike's fees.

   b) Solve the linear system in part a).

   c) Which method for solving linear systems did you use for part b)? Why?

   d) What does your answer in part b) mean?

5. Wendy rented a car for 6 days and drove it 480 km. The rental cost Wendy $361.50. Charles rented the same car for 2 days and drove it 300 km. His rental cost $173.00. Write a linear system for the car rental costs and solve by graphing on a graphing calculator.

Chapter 5 Review

1. Is (5, 3) the solution to each of the given linear systems?
   Explain your answer.
   a) $3x - 4y = 3$ and $x + y = 8$

   b) $x - y - 2 = 0$ and $y = -x - 3$

5.1 Solve Linear Systems by Graphing, textbook pages 198–204

2. Solve each system of linear equations by graphing.
   a) $y = 2x + 3$ and $y = x + 4$ b) $y = 3x - 4$ and $y = x - 2$

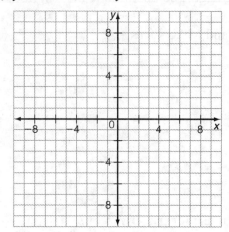 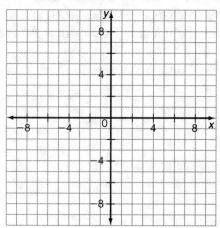

   The solution is (___, ___).   The solution is (___, ___).

3. Use a graphing calculator to solve each linear system.
   a) $y = 2x - 27$ and $y = -x + 12$

   The solution is (___, ___).

   b) $y = 4x + 20$ and $y = 2x + 30$

   The solution is (___, ___).

   c) Why is it easier to solve the linear systems in this question with a graphing calculator than by drawing a graph by hand?

   _____

4. Rearrange each linear equation to isolate y.

    a) $x - y + 4 = 0$ **b)** $2x - 3y - 5 = 0$ **c)** $12x + 4y = 20$

Chapter 5 Review

5.2 Solve Linear Systems by Substitution, textbook pages 205–211

5. A high school student council is selling sweatshirts to raise money for their school. The supplier will charge a $250 flat fee plus $10 per sweatshirt made. The student council wants to sell the sweatshirts for $20 each, but needs to know how many sweatshirts they must sell in order to break even. Show how they could determine this.

    a) For the student council to break even, what does the total cost of having the sweatshirts made need to be equal to?

    b) Write an equation that models the costs of having the sweatshirts made.

    c) Write an equation that models the revenue that the student council will make by selling the sweatshirts for $20 each.

    d) Solve the linear system using your equations from parts **b)** and **c)**.

    e) What is your solution from part **d)**? How many sweatshirts does the student council need to sell to break even?

5.3 Solve Linear Systems by Elimination, textbook pages 212–218

6. Describe what must be done first to solve the system of linear equations $x - 2y = 1$ ① and $x + y = 4$ ②.

    a) If x is to be eliminated: _____

    b) If y is to be eliminated: _____

5.4 Solve Problems Involving Linear Systems, textbook pages 219–227

7. Solve the linear system algebraically, using the elimination or substitution method. Briefly describe why you chose the method that you did.

    $y = 2x + 1$ ① $3x - 5y = 9$ ②

Method used:

Reason:

CHAPTER 6 Quadratic Relations

Get Set

Answer these questions to check your understanding of the Get Ready concepts on pages 236–237 of the *Foundations of Mathematics 10* textbook.

Evaluating Expressions

1. Substitute the given x-value and then solve.

   a) $2x^2 - 12$, $x = 4$ b) $3x^2 - 10x + 50$, $x = -2$

Linear Relations

2. For each relation, complete the table of values and graph the relation.

   a) $y = 3x - 5$

x	y
–3	
–2	
–1	
0	
1	
2	
3	

   b) $y = -x - 2$

x	y
–3	
–2	
–1	
0	
1	
2	
3	

3. State the x- and y-intercepts for each graphed relation.

   a)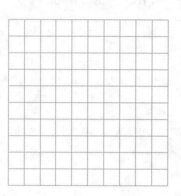

   x-intercept:

   _____

   y-intercept:

   _____

   b)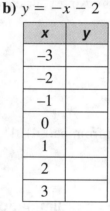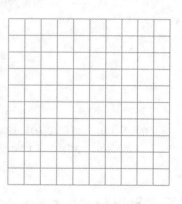

   x-intercept:

   _____

   y-intercept:

   _____

Lines of Symmetry

4. Write the number of lines of symmetry for each shape. Then draw the lines of symmetry for each.

   a)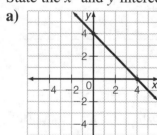

   Number of lines

   of symmetry: _____

   b)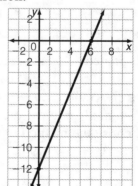

   Number of lines

   of symmetry: _____

6.1 Explore Non-Linear Relations

Textbook
pp. 238–244

Warm-Up

1. Math Literacy	**2. Number Sense**
What type of graph is a parabola? A parabola is a _____ _____ _____ graph.	Draw a line from the type of relation to the correct term. linear relation non-linear relation curve of best fit line of best fit
3. Fractions	**4. Area**

Multiply the following.
 	
 a) $\frac{1}{2}(4) =$
 	
 b) $\frac{1}{2}(12)(3) =$
	Identify the length and width of this rectangle. Then, find the area.
	
	 Length: _____ cm 5 cm
	                2 cm
	 Width: _____ cm
	
	 $A =$ _____ × _____
	
	    =
	
	    =

5. Perimeter	**6. Multiplication**

Calculate the perimeter   12 m
 of this rectangle.   5 m
 	
 $P =$ _____ × _____
 	
   =
 	
   =
 	
   =
	Multiply the following.
	 a) $12 \times 4 =$
	
	 b) $5 \times 9 =$

7. Non-Linear Relations	**8. Relations and Functions**
What is one type of non-linear relation? One type of non-linear relation is a _____ relation.	What is a graph of a quadratic relation called? Circle the correct answer. A graph of a quadratic relation is called a curve of best fit, a line of best fit, or a parabola.

Practise

1. Graph the data in each table. Draw a line or curve of best fit.
   Explain your choice.

a)

x	y
0	3
1	5
2	7
3	9
4	11
5	13

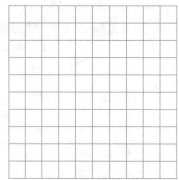

The points _____ (lie, do not lie) in a line, so I drew a _____ (line, curve) of best fit.

b)

x	y
0	0
2	8
4	32
6	72
8	128
10	200

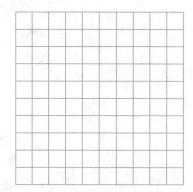

The points _____ (lie, do not lie) in a line, so I drew a _____ (line, curve) of best fit.

2. The relation $SA = 6s^2$ represents the formula for the surface area of a cube with a side length of s.
   a) Find the surface area of a cube with a side length from 1 cm to 6 cm. Record the surface area values in the table.
   b) Graph the data in the table. Draw a curve of best fit through the points. Label your graph completely.

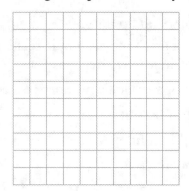

Side Length (cm)	Surface Area (cm²)
1	
2	
3	
4	
5	
6	

3. David has 30 m of fencing to create as large a dog run as possible.

a) The formula to calculate perimeter is $P =$ _____.

The formula to calculate area is $A =$ _____.

b) Complete the table using various lengths and widths for a dog run with a perimeter of 30 m. Change the length and width by 1 m each time.

Length (m)							
Width (m)							
Area (m²)							

c) Graph the data for the area related to width.

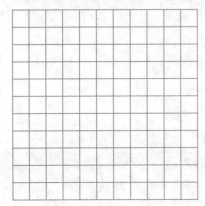

d) The relation between area and width is _____ because_____.

4. The first four figures in a pattern are given below.

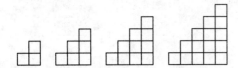

Complete the table for the first six figures that would be in the sequence. Some entries have been filled in.

Figure	Base	Height	Area
1	2	2	3
2	3	3	6
3	4	4	10
4			15
5			
6			

6.2 Model Quadratic Relations

Textbook
pp. 245–253

Warm-Up

1. Number Sense

A quadratic relation can be modelled by an equation in the form of

$y =$ _____ + _____ + _____

The coefficient of the squared term can never be what number?

It can never be _____.

2. Math Literacy

Which of the following are quadratic relations? Circle all that apply.

a) $y = x^2$ **b)** $y = 2x^2 - 8$

c) $y = 2x^2 + 5x + 2$

3. Mental Math

If you joined the following points, would they form a line of best fit or a curve of best fit?

They would

form a _____

of best fit.

Join the points to check your answer.

4. Tables

Plot the following points on the graph.

x	y
−2	4
−1	1
0	0
1	1
2	4

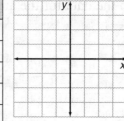

5. Relations and Functions

Rearrange the following equations to isolate the y value.

a) $3x = y + 2$

b) $-5 = 4x - y$

6. Algebra

Find the value of y, if $x = 3$.

a) $y = 3x + 5$

b) $2y = 5x + 1$

7. Quadratic Relations

Find the value of y if $x = 2$.
$y = x^2 + 2x - 5$

8. Rounding

Round the following to the nearest tenth.

a) $102.587 =$

b) $25.09 =$

c) $4.152 =$

Practise

1. How is an equation for a quadratic relation different from an equation that represents a linear relation?

_____

2. Does the equation $y = 3x^2 - 4$ represent a linear or quadratic relation? How do you know?

_____

3. a) Use a graphing calculator to graph the data in the table.
   b) What type of relation best represents the data?

   _____

x	y
−3	27
−2	12
−1	3
0	0
1	3
2	12
3	27

4. a) Complete the table using the values for the points indicated in the graph. One coordinate has been filled in for you.

x	y
−5	20

   b) Using a graphing calculator, determine the equation of the curve of best fit.

   The equation for the graph is _____.

   c) What type of relation fits the data? _____

5. The path of a soccer ball was studied and the following data collected.

a) Enter the data on a graphing calculator.

Section
6.2

Time (s)	Height (m)
0	0
1	24.5
2	39.2
3	44.1
4	39.2
5	24.5
6	0

b) The data appear on the graph in the shape of a _____, therefore,

the data forms a _____ relation.

c) The equation of the relation is _____.

6. The data in the table describe the path of a fireworks display launched from a hill into a flat lowland area.

Horizontal distance (m)	Vertical distance (m)
0	0
3	28.13
6	44.91
9	53.52
12	51.75
15	19.21
18	−11.71

a) Enter the data on a graphing calculator, then display the scatter plot.

b) The equation of the quadratic relation is _____.

6.3 # Key Features of Quadratic Relations

 Textbook pp. 254–263

Warm-Up

1. Math Literacy	**2. Graphs**
Rearrange the following equation to isolate the y variable. $-2 - 4x^2 = -y + 15$	Graph the following relation on a graphing calculator. $y = x^2 - 5$
3. Key Features	**4. Quadratic Relations**
Label the vertex and sketch and label the axis of symmetry for this parabola. 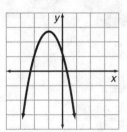	Label the minimum point and the x-intercepts. 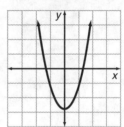
5. Axis of Symmetry	**6. Lines of Symmetry**
Draw the axis of symmetry for the following figure. 	Draw the lines of symmetry for the following. 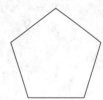
7. Number Sense	**8. Algebra**
Solve for y if $x = 5$. $y = x^2 + 2x - 7$	Rearrange to isolate the y variable. Then solve for y if $x = 3$. $3x^2 + 3y = 6 - 2x$

Practise

1. Draw parabolas that have the following characteristics.

a) a minimum value   **b)** a maximum value   **c)** two *x*-intercepts

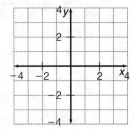   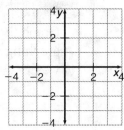   

2. Complete the tables of values using the equations and then graph the data from both tables on the same grid. The first one for each data set has been done for you.

$y = x^2$

x	y
−3	9
−2	
−1	
0	
1	
2	
3	

$y = 2x^2$

x	y
−3	18
−2	
−1	
0	
1	
2	
3	

Sample calculation: $y = x^2$
$y = (-3)^2$
$y = 9$

Sample calculation: $y = x^2$
$y = 2(-3)^2$
$y = 18$

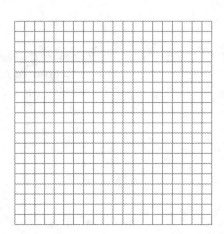

3. Compare the graphs you generated in question 2.
   a) Write down ways they are similar and different.

Section 6.3

   Similarities: _____

   _____

   Differences: _____

   _____

   b) What do you think was the reason for the difference between the graphs?

   _____

   _____

   c) How would the graphs in question 2 change if the sign of the coefficients of the x^2 terms for each equation were negative?

   Changing the sign of the coefficient of x^2 would cause the graphs to _____.

4. Use a graphing calculator to graph the relation $y = -2x^2 + 3x + 5$, then complete the statements.

   a) The coordinates of the vertex are (___, ___) because _____

   _____.

   b) The equation of the axis of symmetry is _____ because _____

   _____.

   c) The y-intercept is _____ because _____.

   d) The x-intercepts are _____ because _____.

   e) Does this graph have a minimum value or a maximum value? What is that value?

   _____

6.4 # Rates of Change in Quadratic Relations

Textbook
pp. 264–271

Warm-Up

1. Math Literacy	2. Number Sense
Solve for y when $x = -2$. $y = x^2 - 5x + 11$	Circle the quadratic equation. $y = x + 2$ $y = 2x^2 - 4x + 6$

3. Estimation	4. Tables
Estimate the number of diagonals you could draw for this polygon. Draw the diagonals to check your answer. 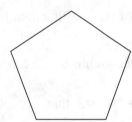	Calculate the first differences for the data below.

x	y	First Differences
-2	4	
-1	1	
0	0	
1	1	

5. Decimals	6. Subtracting Integers
Evaluate the following. $11.2 - 5.9 =$	Subtract the following. $-15 - (-17)$

7. Quadratic Relations	8. Algebra
Rearrange to isolate the y variable. Then solve for y if $x = 4$. $-8 + x + y = 2x^2$	Solve for x. $32 = 2x + 4$

Practise

1. Describe a method that does not involve graphing, which you can use to identify whether data in a table represents a quadratic relation.

   _____

   _____

2. Leon was working on the relation below and filled in the table of values for first and second differences.

x	y	First Differences	Second Differences
−3	5		
−2	7	2	
−1	9	2	0
0	11	2	0
1	13	2	0

   Leon concluded the relation is quadratic because there is a constant value of zero for the second differences. Is he correct? Explain.

   _____

   _____

3. a) Complete the table. The first one has been done for you.

x	y	First Differences	Second Differences
−3	18		
−2	11	11 − 18 = −7	
−1	6	6 − 11 = −5	−5 − (−7) = ____
0	3		
1	2		
2	3		
3	6		

   b) This data forms a _____ relation because _____.

   c) Based on the values you determined for the table, what would the shape of this graph be? Explain why.

   _____

   _____

4. a) Make a table of values for the relation $y = x^2 + 5x + 4$ and use the values in the table to determine whether it is quadratic.

Section
6.4

x	y	First Differences	Second Differences
−5	4	__ − 10 = __	
−4			
−3			
−2			
−1			
0			
1			

Sample calculation:
$y = x^2 + 5x + 4$
$y = (-5)^2 + 5(-5) + 4$
$y = 25 - 25 + 4$
$y = 4$

Calculations:

b) Is the relation quadric? _____. Based on the equation, does this make sense?

Explain. _____

5. This graph shows a quadratic relation.
a) Make a table of values for the graph.

time (s)	height (m)
0	
3	
5	
6	
8	
10	
13	
15	
20	

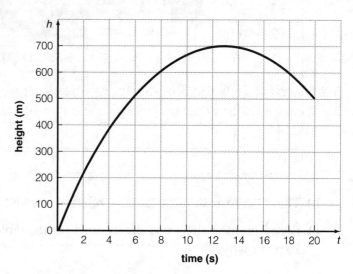

b) Use a graphing calculator to find the expression for this relation.

The equation is_____.

Date: _____

Chapter 6 Review

6.1 Explore Non-Linear Relations, textbook pages 238–244

1. Graph the data in each table. Join the points with a line or a curve of best fit. Explain your choice.

   I used a _____ because

   _____.

x	y
0	2
1	3
2	6
3	11
4	18
5	27
6	38
7	51
8	66

2. The formula for the area of a circle is $A = \pi r^2$, where r represents the radius.

   a) Find the areas of circles for the given radii and record them in the table. Graph the data in the table and connect the data points with a smooth curve. (Use $\pi = 3.14$ for your calculations.)

radius (cm)	Area (cm²)
1	
2	
3	
4	
5	
6	
7	
8	
9	
10	

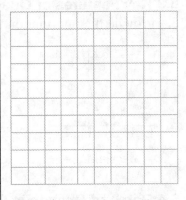

6.2 Model Quadratic Relations, textbook pages 245–253

3. Is each relation linear or quadratic? Explain your answer.

   a) $y = x^2 + 4$

   _____

   b) $y = 3x + 4$

   _____

   c) $y = x^2 + 5x - 6$

   _____

4. Using a graphing calculator, graph the set of data. Describe the type of relation the data set best represents and explain why.

x	y
0	2
0.5	1.25
1	−1
1.5	−4.75
2	−10
2.5	−16.75
3	−25
3.5	−34.75

I think the relation is _____ because _____

_____ .

6.3 Key Features of Quadratic Relations, textbook pages 254–263

5. Provide the information for the graph.

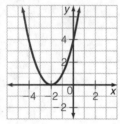

Coordinates of the vertex: (____, ____)

Equation of the axis of symmetry: _____

y-intercept(s): _____

Minimum or maximum value: _____

x-intercept(s): _____

6.4 Rates of Change in Quadratic Relations, textbook pages 264–271

6. Determine if the relation is linear, quadratic, or neither. Provide an explanation for your answer.

x	y	First Differences	Second Differences
−3	12		
−2	7		
−1	4		
0	3		
1	4		
2	7		
3	12		

The relation is _____ because _____ .

CHAPTER 7 Quadratic Expressions

Get Set

Answer these questions to check your understanding of the Get Ready concepts on pages 278–279 of the *Foundations of Mathematics 10* textbook.

Polynomials

1. Circle the numerical coefficient in each term and identify each expression as a monomial, binomial, or trinomial.

   a) $3x$ **b)** $4x^2 + 3x - 1$ **c)** $8x^3$ **d)** $x^2 + 7x$

Algebraic Expressions

2. Multiply or divide as indicated.

   a) $3(4y)$ **b)** $(-2t)(-3t)$ **c)** $-6x \div 3$ **d)** $\dfrac{15x^2}{3x}$

3. Simplify.

   a) $5x + 4 - 7x - 1$ **b)** $x^2 + 2x + 4 + x$ **c)** $x^2 + 8x^2 - 7 - 5x + 13x$

4. Expand.

   a) $2(x - 5)$ **b)** $5x(2x + 6)$ **c)** $-3(4x^2 + 4x - 2)$ **d)** $2x^2(3x + 5)$

Number Operations

5. Square each term.

   a) -6 **b)** $4x$ **c)** $10y$ **d)** $-5x$

Measurement

6. Find the area of the shaded region in the diagram.

20 cm

4 cm

3 cm

15 cm

7.1 Multiply Two Binomials

Textbook pp. 280–289

Warm-Up

1. Number Operations	2. Factors
Evaluate. **a)** $3(2 + 6)$ **b)** $(12 - 6)(10 - 5) + 4$	Find the greatest whole number that divides evenly into each pair. **a)** 8 and 16 **b)** 21 and 49

3. The Distributive Property	4. Math Literacy
Expand. **a)** $4x(3x + 2)$ **b)** $5x(2x + 6)$	**a)** What does the prefix *bi* mean? **b)** Give an example of a word with this prefix.

5. Estimation	6. Simplify Algebraic Expressions
A piece of string 8.2 m long is lengthened by a factor of 4.1. What is the approximate length of the new string?	Simplify. **a)** $14x + 12 - 5x + 8$ **b)** $-(a + 5) + 4a + 7$

Practise

1. a) Write an example of a binomial expression that contains a variable and a constant.

b) Explain your answer for **a)**.

2. Use algebra tiles to illustrate each product of the binomials.

a) $(x + 2)(x + 5)$

b) $(2a + 1)(a + 4)$

3. Use a multiplication pattern to determine the products of the binomials. The order for multiplying terms in binomials is indicated for the first example and is represented by the acronym FOIL.

a) $(x + 6)(x + 3)$

$$= x(x) + x(\underline{}) + 6(\underline{}) + \underline{}(\underline{})$$
$$= x^2 + \underline{}x + \underline{}$$

b) $(2x - 3)(x - 10)$

c) $(a - 9)(7a + 6)$

4. a) Use algebra tiles to find the product of $(x + 3)(x + 3)$.

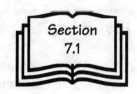

Section
7.1

b) What is another way of writing the binomial in **a)**?

c) What shape did you construct in **a)**?

d) What term is used to describe the resulting expression in **a)**?

5. Rajeet would like to paint a wall in his bedroom and needs
to figure out how much paint he has to buy.
The height and length of the wall can be represented as

a) Find a quadratic expression that represents the
area of the wall.

Area = length × width

Therefore,

Area = (_____) × (_____)

$= ___ x^2 + ___ x + ___ x + ___$

$=$

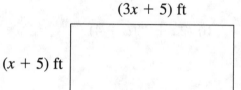

$(3x + 5)$ ft

$(x + 5)$ ft

b) Find the area of the wall if $x = 3$.

6. Use the distributive property of multiplication to determine the product of the following
binomials.
$(3x + 2)(x + 2)$

$= ___ x^2 + ___ x + ___ x + ___$

$=$

7. Use a CAS to determine the product of the following binomials.
$(4x + 3)(x + 2)$

So, $(4x + 3)(x + 2) =$ _____

7.2 Common Factoring

Textbook
pp. 290–297

Warm-Up

1. Number Operations	2. Factors
Evaluate. **a)** $\dfrac{(3 \times 4)}{2} + \dfrac{(3 \times 9)}{3}$ **b)** $-(-2 \times 9) \div 3$	Provide three factors of **a)** 30 **b)** 72

3. The Distributive Property	4. Math Literacy
Expand. **a)** $2a(6 - 2a + b)$ **b)** $-7(x - 4y + 6)$	What is the opposite process to factoring? Explain why.

5. Estimate	6. Simplify Algebraic Expressions
A case of printer paper containing 5 packages of 500 sheets costs $24.89. **a)** Roughly how much does each package of paper cost? **b)** Roughly how much does each sheet of paper cost?	Simplify. **a)** $-4x + 4 - 12x - 6$ **b)** $x^2 + 2x + 4 + x + 4x^2$

Practise

1. Find the greatest common factor (GCF) of
   a) 64 and 72   b) $2a^2$ and $12a$ c) $4x^2$ and $6x$

2. For each polynomial, indicate if it is in the *factored* form or *expanded* form and identify the greatest common factor.
   a) $3x - 12$ b) $5(13y - x^2)$ c) $3x^2 - 12x + 9$

   GCF =   GCF =   GCF =

3. Completely factor each polynomial and check by expanding
   a) $3p - 15$ b) $21x^2 - 9x + 18$ c) $6y^2 + 18y + 30$

   $= 3(\underline{} - \underline{})$ $=$ $=$

   Check: **Check:**   **Check:**

4. Write a trinomial expression with a GCF of $3n$. Factor the expression.

5. The expression $A = 5x^2 + 15x$ represents the area of a playground in a
    park, with area in square metres (m^2).

    a) Factor the expression completely.

    $A = $ ___(___ + ___)

    b) Based on your answer for part **a)**, provide expressions for the dimensions and draw a
    sketch of the playground.

    c) What is the area of the playground if $x = 9$ m?

    d) The city has decided to completely fence in the playground and needs to determine its
    perimeter. Using the dimensions from part **b)**, write the formulas for the perimeter and
    area of the playground.

    Perimeter = 2_____ + 2_____

    Area = _____ _____

    e) Using the area you calculated in **c)**, determine how many metres of fencing will be
    needed to completely fence in the playground.

6. Use a CAS to find the GCF for the following trinomials.
    a) $6a^2 + 12a + 18$

    GCF = _____

    b) $18a^2 + 27a + 81$

    GCF = _____

7.3 Factor a Difference of Squares

Textbook
pp. 298–305

Warm-Up

1. Number Operations	2. Factors
Evaluate. **a)** $(6)^2 - (-2)^2$ **b)** $(-3)^2 - (1)^2$	**a)** Circle the common factors of 16 and 36 2, 3, 4, 6, 8, 9, 16, 18 **b)** Which number from **a)** is the greatest common factor?

3. Algebra	4. Math Literacy
Expand. **a)** $4(t^2 - 4)$ **b)** Is your answer for **a)** a difference of squares?	Circle the example of a difference of squares. **a)** $5^2 - 3$ **b)** $100 - 50$ **c)** $49 - x^2$ **d)** $x^2 - x$

5. Estimate	6. Algebraic Expressions
Estimate the value of 11.1^2.	**a)** Simplify $3x^2 + (6)^2 - 2x^2$ **b)** Evaluate part **a)** when $x = 3$

Practise

1. Write each as a power of its positive square root.
   a) 64
   b) 144
   c) $9x^2$

2. Identify the expressions that are differences of squares. Explain your answers.
   a) $x^2 - 49$
   b) $4x^2 - 4y^2$
   c) $9x^2 - 5y$

   _____

   _____

3. Factor each expression and check by expanding.
   a) $x^2 - 9$
   STEP 1: Both terms are square terms and the operation between them is subtraction, so you are factoring a difference of squares. Each term can be written as a power of its positive square root.

   $= x^2 - 3^2$

   STEP 2: Write the binomials that represent the factors.

   $= (x + \underline{\quad})(\underline{\quad} - \underline{\quad})$

   Check:

   b) $100 - x^2$

   Check:

   c) $a^2 - 81$

   Check:

4. a) Using a ruler, draw a square with sides measuring 6 cm.

b) Determine the area of the square.

A = _____ × _____

=

c) Is it possible to represent the calculation in part **a)** as a squared number? Explain.

d) Inside of the large square, draw another square with sides measuring 2 cm and calculate its area.

e) Determine the remaining area of the large square if you were to cut out the small square.

f) How is the calculation in part **e)** related to determining a difference of squares?

5. The area of a $5 bill can be modelled by the expression A = $x^2 - 16$, with area in square centimetres.
   a) Find the expressions for length and width.
      You can find them by factoring the equation for area. Therefore,

   A = (   )(   )

   b) Determine what x is, to the nearest centimetre, by measuring a $5 bill.

   c) What is the area of the $5 bill?

   d) Check your answer to part **c)** by substituting the value of x into A = $x^2 - 16$.

Date: _____

 7.4 Factor Trinomials of the Form $x^2 + bx + c$

Textbook
pp. 306-311

Warm-Up

1. Number Operations	2. Factors
Evaluate. **a)** $24 - (4 \times 2 + 2 \times 9)$ **b)** $22 \times 3 - (-2)(1)$	Find the greatest common factor for the expressions in each pair. **a)** $3x^2$ and 9 **b)** $4x$ and $6xy$
3. Algebra	**4. Math Literacy**
Expand. **a)** $7(x^2 - 2x + 6)$ **b)** $4b(b - 7)$	Give two examples of careers that require knowing how to calculate areas.
5. Estimate	**6. Algebraic Expressions**
The distance between Toronto and North Bay is about 345 km. If you travel at an average speed of 80 km/h, about how long will it take you to get there? **a)** 3 h **b)** 4 h **c)** 5 h **d)** 6 h	Simplify. **a)** $-2b + 6 + 7b^2 + 7 - b^2$ **b)** Evaluate part **a)** when $b = 2$

Practise

1. Complete the table by determining the appropriate pair of integers whose product and sum are as listed.

Pair of Integers	Product	Sum
	8	6
	36	13
	−20	−1
	24	−10

2. **a)** Use algebra tiles to construct a rectangle with area $x^2 + 6x + 8$.
   b) Based on your model, what expressions represent the length and width for this rectangle?

   c) How do the length and width of your rectangle relate to the factors for the trinomial expression?

3. Factor each trinomial and check by expanding.
   a) $x^2 + 4x + 3$

   STEP 1: Find a pair of integers that have a product of 3 and a sum of 4.
   The product is positive, so both integers are either negative or positive.

   Since their sum is 4 the integers must be _____ and _____.

   STEP 2: Determine the binomial factors.

   $(x +$ ___$)($___ $+$ ___$)$

   Check:

   b) $x^2 + 11x + 28$ **c)** $x^2 + 9x + 20$

   Check: **Check:**

4. Nancy is factoring $x^2 - 6x + 8$ and decides that she will use 4 and 2 as her values so that the expression becomes $(x + 4)(x + 2)$. Explain where a mistake was made.

Section
7.4

5. A rectangle has an area $x^2 + 8x + 7$.
a) What are the expressions that could represent the dimensions of the rectangle?

$A = ($ $)($ $)$

b) What is the name of the process you performed to get the expressions in part **a)**?

c) What is the area of this rectangle when $x = 9$ cm?

6. An interior designer wants to develop a floor plan of a room with the area $x^2 + 6x + 9$.
a) Factor to find the dimensions of the room. Explain your answer.

b) What is the area of the room if $x = 1$ m?

c) Draw and label a diagram of the room.

Chapter 7 Review

7.1 Multiply Two Binomials, textbook pages 280–289

1. Expand and simplify.
   a) $(2x - 1)(3x + 4)$

   b) $(x + 7)(2x - 2)$

   c) $(x - 3)(3x + 1)$

   d) $(x - 1)^2$

7.2 Common Factoring, textbook pages 290–297

2. Expand.
   a) $(x - 3)(x + 3)$

   b) $(x + 3)^2$

   c) What do you notice about your answers? Explain.

3. Determine if the following expressions are factored completely. If they are not, write the correctly factored form.
   a) $3x^2 + 12x$
      $= x(3x + 12)$

   b) $18x^3 + 6x^2$
      $= 2x(9x^2 + 3x)$

4. Find the greatest common factor, if necessary, then factor each expression completely.
   a) $2x^2 + 20$

   b) $4x^2y + 8xy$

c) $x^2 - 144$ **d)** $x^2 - 5x - 14$

Chapter 7
Review

7.3 Factor a Difference of Squares, textbook pages 298–305

5. Write each number as a power of its positive square root.

   a) $25 =$ _____   **b)** $49 =$ _____   **c)** $81 =$ _____

6. Circle the difference of squares.

   a) $x^2 - 64$ **b)** $4x^2 - 100$ **c)** $x - 25$ **d)** $x^2 + 49$

7. Factor each difference of squares.

   a) $x^2 - 9$ **b)** $x^2 - 16$

Check: **Check:**

7.4 Factor Trinomials of the Form $x^2 + bx + c$, textbook pages 306–311

8. A carpenter is installing a countertop with an area $x^2 + 7x + 6$.

   a) Write expressions for the length and width of the countertop.

   b) What is the shape of the countertop?

   c) Calculate the area of the countertop if $x = 1$ ft.

CHAPTER 8

Represent Quadratic Relations

Get Set

Answer these questions to check your understanding of the Get Ready concepts on pages 318-319 of the *Foundations of Mathematics 10* textbook.

Relations

1. Graph the relation, then identify the relation as linear, quadratic, or neither.

   _____

x	y
−4	0
−3	−12
−2	−20
−1	−24
0	−24
1	−20
2	−12
3	0

Key Features of Quadratic Relations

2. Identify the information indicated.

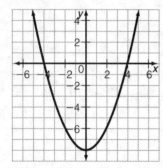

Coordinates of vertex: (____, ____)

Equation of axis of symmetry: _____

x-intercepts: _____

y-intercept: _____

Algebraic Operations

3. Substitute each given value for x, then solve for y.

   a) $y = (x - 3)^2 + 1$ for $x = 2$: _____

   b) $y = 2x^2 + 5x + 5$ for $x = -3$: _____

4. Expand and simplify.
   a) $(x - 4)^2$ **b)** $(x + 4)(x - 1)$

5. Factor.
   a) $4x^2 - 12$ **b)** $x^2 - 7x + 10$

8.1 Interpret Quadratic Relations

Textbook pp. 320–328

Warm Up

1. Linear Systems
Solve the linear system $y = 2x + 3$ and $y = -x + 12$.

2. Identify Quadratic Relations

Use first and second differences to determine if the relation is quadratic.

x	y	First Differences	Second Differences
−3	20		
−2	13		
−1	8		
0	5		
1	4		
2	5		
3	8		

3. Graph Quadratic Relations

Graph the relation $y = \frac{1}{2}x^2 - 4$.

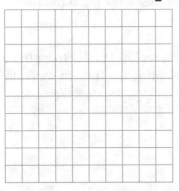

4. Algebraic Operations

Re-arrange each equation into slope and y-intercept form.

a) $x + y - 3 = 0$ **b)** $4x - 2y + 5 = 0$

5. Math Literacy

Explain how to determine if two lines are parallel or perpendicular. Include an example of each situation.

_____

_____

6. Common Factoring

Factor completely.
$3a^3 - 15a$

7. Factor Trinomials

Factor $x^2 - x - 2$.

8. Substitute and Solve

Given the equation $y = 3x^2 - 4$, find the value of y when $x = -2$.

Practise: Interpret Quadratic Relations

Section
8.1

1. The graph shows the path that a rugby ball followed after it was kicked. The y-axis represents the height of the ball in metres while the x-axis represents the horizontal position of the ball in metres.

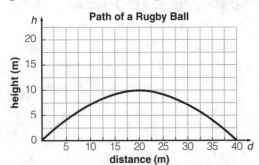

a) What was the maximum height reached by the ball? _____

b) At what horizontal distance did the ball reach its maximum height? _____

c) How far did the ball travel before it hit the ground? _____

d) If the kicker was 32 m out from the cross bar of a goal post, would the ball pass over the cross bar if it is 3 m off of the ground? _____

e) What is the farthest distance the ball can be kicked and still pass over the 3 m cross bar?

_____

2. The quadratic relation $h = -5t^2 + 210$ describes the path of a rock that falls from the top of a cliff, with h representing the height in metres and t representing the time in seconds.

a) Complete the table. Then graph the relation.
   $h = -5t^2 + 210$

t (s)	h (m)
0	
1	
2	
3	
4	
5	
6	

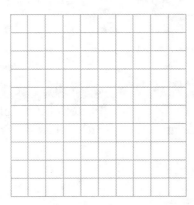

b) What is the height of the cliff? _____

c) How long will it take the rock to reach the bottom of the cliff?

Round your answer to the nearest tenth of a second. _____

d) How far from the bottom of the cliff is the rock when half of the time has passed?

_____

3. The table shows the curve of a clothes line that hangs between two poles 35 m apart.

Horizontal Distance from First Pole (m)	0	5	10	15	20	25	30	35
Height of Line Above Ground (m)	2.14	1.77	1.52	1.49	1.46	1.51	1.73	2.12

a) Use a graphing calculator to plot the data.

b) Find the equation that models the curve of the clothes line. _____

c) Answer to the nearest tenth of a metre. How far from the ground is the lowest point?

_____

At what horizontal distance does it occur? _____

d) How far from each end could a person 1.6 m tall stand so their head just touches the line?

_____

4. Describe two methods that can be used to determine if a relation is quadratic.

_____

_____

_____

5. A harbour ferry service has 240 000 riders per month who pay a fare of $2. The fare is to increase in the new year. Previous fare increases have shown that for every $0.10 increase in the fare, the number of riders will drop by 10 000.

a) Complete the table.

Fare ($)	Riders	Total Revenue ($)
2.00	240 000	480 000
2.10		
2.20		
2.30		
2.40		
2.50		
2.60		

b) Plot revenue versus fare using a graphing calculator.

c) What fare price would generate the most revenue? _____

d) What total revenue would this generate? _____

8.2 # Represent Quadratic
Relations in Different Ways

Textbook
pp. 329–335

Warm Up

1. Linear Systems

State the point of intersection.

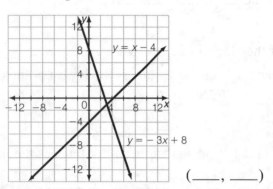

(___ , ___)

2. Quadratic Relations

Complete a table of values from
$x = -3$ to $x = 3$ for the relation
$y = 3x^2 - 3x - 6$.

x							
y							

3. Solve a Linear System Algebraically

Solve the linear system
$y = x + 2$ and
$y = -x - 8$.

4. Math Literacy

Explain how you could show that the
relations $y = (x - 2)(x + 1)$ and
$y = x^2 - x - 2$ are different forms
of the same equation, using a graphing
calculator.

_____

_____

_____

_____

_____

5. Factor Trinomials

Factor completely.
$x^2 - 9x + 8$

6. Identify the x-Intercepts

What are the x-intercepts of the relation
$y = (x - 3)(x + 6)$?

7. Compare Quadratic Equations

Do the equations $y = x^2 + x - 6$ and
$y = (x - 3)(x + 2)$ represent the same
relation? How do you know?

8. Analyze a Quadratic Relation

Given the equation $y = x^2 + 7x + 6$,
identify the x- and y-intercepts.

Practise: Represent Quadratic Relations in Different Ways

Section
8.2

1. Find the x-intercepts of each quadratic relation without graphing.

   a) $y = x^2 - 3x - 28$

   b) $y = c^2 + 2c - 15$

   c) $y = x^2 + x - 12$

2. Identify the y-intercept of each quadratic relation.

   a) $y = -x^2 + 2$

   b) $y = 3x^2 - 6x - 4$

   c) $y = -3x^2 + 4x - 6$

3. Explain how you can determine whether a quadratic relation will have a minimum or a maximum value, without graphing the relation.

   _____

   _____

   _____

4. The area of a rectangle can be represented by the relation $A = 8x - x^2$.

   a) Factor the expression for area. _____

   b) What value of x will generate the rectangle with the greatest area? _____

x (cm)									
Area (cm²)									

   c) What will be the greatest area? _____

5. A rectangle has dimensions $x + 11$ and $2x + 5$, both measured in centimetres.
   a) Draw the rectangle and label the sides.
   b) Write the area inside the rectangle.

   _____

   c) Find the value of x that will produce an area of 117 cm².

> Section
> 8.2

> **Hint**: this means that the year 2000 is $t = 0$ and 2003 would be $t = 3$.

6. A model for the population in a small city is given by the relation $P = 14t^2 + 820t + 42\,000$, where t is the time in years measured from the year 2000.
   a) Calculate what the population will be in 2009.

   b) Calculate what the population was in 1997.

   c) Graph the relation $P = 14t^2 + 820t + 42\,000$ using a graphing calculator.

   d) Find when the population was the least. _____

   e) What was the least population? _____

7. The path of a soccer ball can be defined by the relation $h = -0.025d^2 + d$, where h represents the height in metres and d represents the horizontal distance in metres the ball travels before it hits the ground.

   a) Find the d-intercepts. _____

   b) Sketch a graph of the relation.

distance (m)								
height (m)								

   c) What is the maximum height of the soccer ball? _____

   d) How far will the soccer ball have travelled horizontally at its maximum height?

   _____

Date: _____

 8.3 The Quadratic Relation
$$y = ax^2 + c$$

Textbook
pp. 336–343

Warm Up

1. Linear Systems

Solve the linear system.
$y = 4x - 5$
$y = x + 1$

2. Quadratic Relations

Complete the table of values for the relation.

$y = x^2 + 3x + 2$

x	−5	−4	−3	−2	−1	0	1	2	3	4	5
y											

3. Quadratic Relations

Complete the table of values for the relation.

$y = (x + 1)(x + 2)$

x	−5	−4	−3	−2	−1	0	1	2	3	4	5
y											

4. Graph Quadratic Relations

Graph the relations $y = x^2 + 3x + 2$ and $y = (x + 1)(x + 2)$ on the same grid.

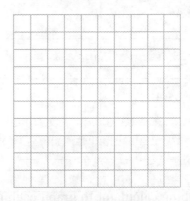

5. Math Literacy

Refer to the graphs from question 4. Explain why the graphs look the way they do.

6. Compare Quadratic Relations

Which of these equations represent parabolas that open downward? How do you know?

a) $y = 3x^2 - 6$

b) $y = -x^2 + 3$

c) $y = -\dfrac{1}{2}x^2$

7. Manipulate Quadratic Equations

The graph of the quadratic relation $y = -3x^2 + c$ passes through the point $(1, 2)$. Find the value of c.

8. Manipulate Quadratic Equations

The graph of the quadratic relation $y = ax^2 - 26$ passes through the point $(3, 1)$. Find the value of a.

Practise: The Quadratic Relation $y = ax^2 + c$

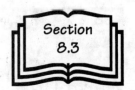

Section
8.3

1. Without graphing, order the quadratic relations from narrowest to widest.

   a) i) $y = \dfrac{1}{2}x^2 + 3$ **ii)** $y = x^2 + 3$ **iii)** $m = 2p^2 + 3$

   Order: _____

   b) i) $y = -\dfrac{1}{4}x^2 - 4$ **ii)** $r = -\dfrac{1}{2}s^2 - 4$ **iii)** $y = -\dfrac{1}{3}x^2 - 4$

   Order: _____

2. For each quadratic relation, find the y-intercept and determine if it is a minimum or a maximum value.

Quadratic Relation	y-intercept	Maximum or Minimum
a) $y = x^2 + 5$		
b) $y = -\dfrac{1}{3}x^2 - 7$		
c) $y = -3x^2 + 27$		
d) $y = \dfrac{1}{4}x^2 - 1$		

3. Use a graphing calculator to graph each relation in question 2, then find the x-intercepts of each relation.

   a) _____   **b)** _____   **c)** _____   **d)** _____

4. A penny is dropped into a tank of water at the water's surface. It falls to the bottom according to the relation $d = -3.5t^2 + 35$, where d is the depth of the water measured in metres and t is the time after the penny was dropped, measured in seconds.

time (s)	depth (m)
0	
1	

   a) Complete the table of values for the relation $d = -3.5t^2 + 35$. Round your answer to one decimal place.

   b) How deep is the tank of water? _____

   c) How long will it take for the penny to reach the bottom of the tank?

   _____

5. Graph each pair of quadratic relations on the same grid and describe the graphs.

Section 8.3

a) $y = 2(x + 3)(x - 3)$ and
$y = 2x^2 - 18$

b) $y = -4x^2 + 4$ and
$y = -4(x - 1)(x + 1)$

x	y
−4	

x	y

x	y
−3	

x	y

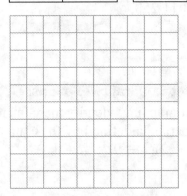

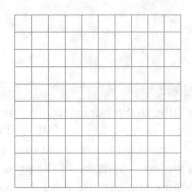

_____

_____

_____

_____

6. A square room of side length 8 m contains a square carpet of side length $2x$ m centred in the room.

a) Draw a diagram modelling the floor of the room.

b) What is the area of the floor of the room?

_____

c) What is the area of the square carpet?

_____

d) Write an expression to represent the area of the bare floor that surrounds the carpet.

_____

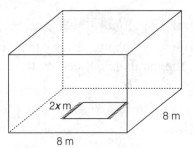

2x m

8 m

8 m

8.4 Solve Problems Involving Quadratic Relations

Textbook
pp. 344–351

Warm Up

1. Factor Trinomials Factor $x^2 + 5x - 14$.	**2. Quadratic Relations** Graph the relations below on the same set of axes using a graphing calculator. $y = -2x^2 + 3x + 9$ $y = (x - 3)(2x + 3)$
3. Factor a Difference of Squares Factor $4h^2 - 81$.	**4. Interpret Quadratic Relations** Use technology to identify the maximum or minimum of the quadratic relation defined by the equation $a = -45b^2 + 750c + 11\ 250$.
5. Math Literacy The equation that models the revenue for a product is $R = -38x^2 + 500x + 2500$, where R represents the revenue in dollars and x represents the price of the product. Explain how you can use the equation to determine the price that gives the maximum revenue.	**6. Interpret Quadratic Relations** Without graphing, identify the y-intercept of the parabola defined by the equation $y = (x + 2)(x - 9)$.
7. Interpret Quadratic Relations Without graphing, identify the x-intercepts of the parabola defined by the equation $y = x^2 - 16$.	**8. Trajectory of a Rocket** A model rocket follows a path described by the relation $h = -5t^2 + 200t$, with h representing the height in metres and t the time in seconds after the rocket was fired. **a)** How long is the rocket in the air? _____ **b)** When does it reach its maximum height? _____

Practise: Solve Problems Involving Quadratic Relations

Section
8.4

1. The path of a basketball can be modelled by the relation $h = -0.06d^2 + 0.6d + 3$, where h is the height of the ball in metres and d is the horizontal distance the ball travels in metres.

   a) Find the maximum height reached by the ball using technology.

   _____

   b) What is the horizontal distance the ball has travelled when it reaches this maximum height?

   _____

distance (m)	height (m)

2. On the set for an upcoming movie, a stunt woman jumped from a window of a burning building. The path followed by the stunt woman can be modelled by the relation $h = -4.9t^2 + 71.7$, where h is her height, in metres, above the safety net and t is the time, in seconds, since she jumped.

   a) How far below the window is the safety net?

   _____

   b) Calculate how far the stunt woman falls in the first 1.6 s after jumping. Round your answer to three decimal places.

   c) Calculate how long it will take her to fall to the safety net. Round your answer to two decimal places.

3. Jeremy kicked a football that follows a path that can be modelled by the relation $h = -4.9t^2 + 26t + 0.25$, where h represents the height, in metres, and t represents the time, in seconds, after Jeremy kicked the ball. Round your answers to two decimal places.

   a) Find the zeros of the relation using a graphing calculator. Interpret their meaning.

   _____

   b) How long after the ball was kicked did it reach its maximum height?

   _____

   c) What is the maximum height? _____

4. A baseball hit by a batter follows a path that can be described by the quadratic relation $h = -5t^2 + 10t + 1$, where h represents the height, in metres, and t represents the time, in seconds, after the ball was hit.

Section
8.4

a) Complete the table of values for the relation.

$h = -5t^2 + 10t + 1$

time (s)	0	0.5	1	1.5	2	2.5	3
height (m)							

b) How high off the ground was the ball when it was hit? _____

c) What was the maximum height of the ball? _____

   How long did it take for the ball to reach its maximum height? _____

d) Calculate the total time the ball was in the air to the nearest tenth of a second.

5. The organizers of a spring fair have developed a profit relation (P) that depends on the ticket price (t) charged per person. The profit is modelled using the relation $P = -37t^2 + 1258t - 7700$.

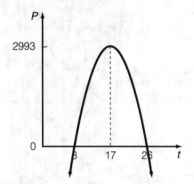

a) What does the third term represent in this relation? _____

b) Find the ticket price that would produce a maximum profit. _____

c) What will be the maximum profit? _____

Chapter 8 Review

8.1 Interpret Quadratic Relations

1. The data in the table represent the path of a disc after it was thrown into the air.

   a) Use a graphing calculator. Graph the data and find the curve of best fit.

   b) How far did the disc travel horizontally before it hit the ground? Round your answer to one decimal place. _____

   c) What was the disc's maximum height? Round your answer to one decimal place.

   _____

Horizontal Distance (ft)	Height (ft)
0	0.8
10	5.0
20	13.4
30	20.0
40	22.7
50	23.5
60	22.4
70	19.8

   d) How far had it travelled horizontally when it reached this height?

   Round your answer to one decimal place. _____

2. A hamburger stand sells a total of 300 hamburgers per day at $3.50 each. Market research has shown that for every $0.25 increase in price, 15 fewer hamburgers will be sold.

   a) Complete the table.

   b) Plot revenue versus price using a graphing calculator.

   c) What price would generate the highest total revenue?

   _____

Price ($)	Number Sold	Revenue ($)
3.50	300	1050
3.75	285	
4.00		
4.25		
4.50		
4.75		
5.00		
5.25		
5.50		

   d) What total revenue would this generate? _____

8.2 Represent Quadratic Relations in Different Ways

Chapter 8
Review

3. Identify the x-intercepts.

   a) $y = x^2 + 5x + 6$ **b)** $y = x^2 - 8x$

   c) $y = x^2 - 4x - 12$ **d)** $y = 12x^2 - 20x$

4. A car rental agency rents 400 cars a week at \$80 per car. Industry research has shown that for every \$2 increase in rental price, an agency will rent 8 fewer cars.

   a) Write an expression for the number of cars rented if the price is raised x times.

     _____

   b) Write an expression for the amount per car if the price is raised x times.

     _____

   c) Multiply the answers for parts **a)** and **b)** to get an expression that represents the revenue.

   d) Find the maximum revenue. _____

   e) For this revenue, how many cars are rented? _____

     What is the rental price per car? _____

5. How can you determine if a quadratic relation of the form $y = ax^2 + bx + c$ is the same as or different from a relation of the form $y = (x - s)(x - t)$?

   _____

   _____

   _____

8.3 The Quadratic Relation $y = ax^2 + c$

6. **a)** Complete the second and third columns in the table without a calculator.

Quadratic Relation	y-Intercept	Maximum or Minimum	x-Intercepts
a) $y = 2x^2 - 32$			
b) $y = \dfrac{1}{3}x^2 - 3$			
c) $y = x^2 + 9$			
d) $y = -\dfrac{3}{4}x^2 - 5$			

Date: _____

b) Graph each relation in part a using a graphing calculator and determine its *x*-intercepts. Fill in the last column of the table with your answers.

7. A roadway on a bridge is supported by two towers with a cable that joins them.

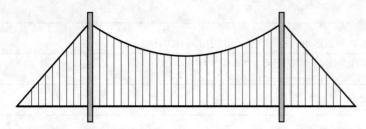

The cables between the towers hang in a parabolic shape that can be represented with the equation $y = 0.00036x^2 + 4$.
a) Graph the relation $y = 0.00036x^2 + 4$ on a graphing calculator.
b) Identify the minimum or maximum value and the coordinates of the vertex.

_____

c) Identify the *y*- and *x*-intercepts.

_____

8.4 Solve Problems Involving Quadratic Relations
8. The cost (in thousands of dollars) to produce items in a computer component manufacturing plant is given by the relation $C = 2x^2 - 29x + 100$, where *x* represents the number of hundreds of items produced. The revenue these items produce (in thousands of dollars) is given by the relation $R = x^2 - 10x + 250$, where *x* represents the number of hundreds of items sold.
a) Profit is defined as the difference between the revenue and the cost. Using $P = R - C$, as well as the two relations above, develop a profit relation for the company.

b) Graph your relation from part a on a graphing calculator.

c) Determine the zeros of the profit relation. _____

d) How many items should be produced to maximize profit? _____

e) What will be the maximum profit? _____

9. The local community theatre group sold 1200 tickets for the holiday concert at $20 per ticket. The committee plans to increase prices this year by $2 per ticket but they also believe that for each $2 increase, 60 fewer tickets will be sold.

Chapter 8
Review

a) Define your variables, then write the revenue relation that describes the ticket sales.

_____

_____

_____

_____

b) Complete the table of values.

Ticket price ($)	20	22							
Tickets sold (n)	1200								
Revenue ($)	24 000								

c) What selling price per ticket should maximize total revenue? _____

d) How many tickets must be sold to reach the maximum total revenue? _____

e) What is the maximum total revenue? _____

CHAPTER 9

Volume and Surface Area

Get Set

Answer these questions to check your understanding of the Get Ready concepts on pages 362–363 of the *Foundations of Mathematics 10* textbook.

Pythagorean Theorem

1. Find the length of the indicated side of this right triangle to one decimal place.

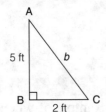

Solution:
The length of the legs are ____ ft and ____ ft.
The length of the hypotenuse is x ft.

$$(\underline{\hspace{1cm}})^2 + (\underline{\hspace{1cm}})^2 = x^2$$

$$\underline{\hspace{1cm}} + \underline{\hspace{1cm}} = x^2$$

$$\underline{\hspace{1cm}} = x^2$$

$$\sqrt{\underline{\hspace{1cm}}} = x$$

$$\underline{\hspace{1cm}} \doteq x$$

The hypotenuse is approximately ____ ft long.

Nets

2. Identify the solid for this net.

The net has a _____ base and _____ congruent

triangular faces. It is a net of a _____.

Convert Measurements

3. Convert each measure to the unit indicated.

852 in. _____ ft   0.084 m _____ mm   0.6 m² _____ cm²   3.4 ft³ _____ in.³

Area

4. Find the area of the circle. Round your answer to one decimal place.

$$A = \pi r^2$$

$$= \pi \times \underline{\hspace{1cm}}$$

$$\doteq \underline{\hspace{1cm}}$$

9.1 **Volume of Prisms and Pyramids**

Textbook pp. 364–371

Warm-Up

1. Pythagorean Theorem	2. Rearrange Formulas
The hypotenuse of a right triangle is 10 in. long. One leg of the triangle is 8 in. long. How long is the other leg?	Rearrange the formula to isolate P. $I = Prt$

3. Rearrange Formulas	4. Math Literacy
Rearrange the formula to isolate t. $d = at^2$	Give an everyday example of when it would be important to determine the volume of an object.

5. Algebraic Equations	6. Alegebraic Equations
Find the value of y when $x = 2$. $y = 3x^2 + 2x - 5$	Find the value of A when $x = 4$ and $y = -2$. $A = 3xy - 4x + 3y$

Practise

Where necessary, round your answers to one decimal place.

1. Find the volume of each prism.

   Area of base = length × width

   A = _____cm × _____cm

   = _____

   The area of the base is _____.

   Volume = area of base × height

   V = _____cm² × _____cm

   = _____

   The volume of the prism is _____.

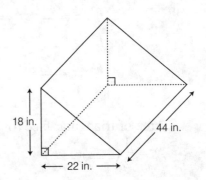

12 cm
15 cm
85 cm

2. Find the volume of the prism.

   Area of triangular face (or base) = $\frac{1}{2}bh$

   A = $\frac{1}{2}$(_____in.)(_____in.)

   = _____

   The area of the triangular face is _____.

   Volume = area of base × height

   V = _____in.² × _____in.

   = _____

   The volume of the prism is _____.

18 in.
22 in.
44 in.

3. Find the volume of the pyramid.

   Area of base = length × width

   A = _____ft × _____ft

   = _____

   The area of the base is _____.

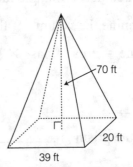

70 ft
20 ft
39 ft

   Volume of pyramid = $\frac{1}{3}$ area of base × height

   V = $\frac{1}{3}$ (_____ft²)(_____ft)

   = _____

   The volume of the pyramid is _____.

4. Find the volume of the prism.

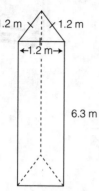

STEP 1: Determine the area of the triangular face, using the Pythagorean theorem to calculate the height. Round your answer to two decimal places.

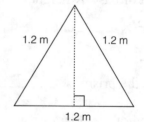

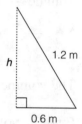

$$\underline{\quad}^2 + h^2 = \underline{\quad}^2$$

$$h^2 = \underline{\quad}^2 - \underline{\quad}^2$$

$$h^2 = \underline{\quad} - \underline{\quad}$$

$$h^2 = \underline{\quad}$$

$$h \doteq \underline{\quad}$$

Area of triangular face (or base) $= \frac{1}{2}bh$

$$A = \frac{1}{2}(\underline{\quad})(\underline{\quad})$$

$$= $$

$$= $$

The Area of the triangle face is _____.

STEP 2: Determine the volume of the prism. Round your answer to three decimal places.

Volume = area of base × height

$$V = \underline{\quad} \times \underline{\quad}$$

$$= \underline{\quad}$$

The volume of the prism is _____.

5. A box in the shape of a rectangular prism has a length of 10 cm, a width of 8 cm, and a height of 5 cm. Find the volume of the box.

9.2 Surface Area of Prisms and Pyramids

Textbook pp. 372–380

Warm-Up

1. Pythagorean Theorem	**2. Math Literacy**
In triangle ABC, angle B measures 90°, the length of side AB is 15 cm, and the length of side BC is 11 cm. Draw the triangle. Use the Pythagorean theorem to find the length of side AC to one decimal place.	Give two examples from real life where you would need to know the surface area of an object.

3. Rearrange Formulas	**4. Algebra**
Rearrange each formula to isolate the indicated variable. **a)** $A = bh$, for h **b)** $C = 2\pi r$, for r	Solve each equation for the given values. **a)** $x = 22y + 11$ for x if $y = 2$ **b)** $y = x^2 + 11$ for y if $x = 5$

5. Nets	**6. Nets**
What object would this net make? 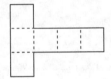	What object would this net make? 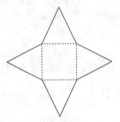

7. Congruence	**8. Math Literacy**
Circle the correct answer. If two triangles are congruent, it means they are **a)** similar **b)** exactly the same size and shape **c)** completely different from each other	Jeremy suggests the Pythagorean theorem can be used to calculate the length of side AB in triangle ABC. Is Jeremy correct? Explain your answer. 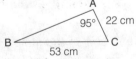

Practise

Where necessary, round your answers to one decimal place.

1. Draw and label a net for the
    rectangular prism.

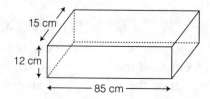

2. Find the surface area of the prism in question 1.

    Two faces have dimensions _____ cm by _____ cm.

    Area = _____ × _____

        = _____

    Two faces have dimensions _____ cm by _____ cm.

    Area = _____ × _____

        = _____

    Two faces have dimensions _____ cm by _____ cm.

    Area = _____ × _____

        = _____

    Surface Area = 2(_____) + 2(_____) + 2(_____)

              = _____

    The surface area of the prism is _____ cm².

3. Draw and label a net for this square-based pyramid.

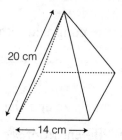

4. Find the surface area of the pyramid in question 3.

Section 9.2

STEP 1: Find the height of each triangular face of the pyramid using Pythagorean theorem. Round your answer to two decimal places.

$h^2 +$ _____ $=$ _____

$h^2 =$ _____ $-$ _____

$h^2 = \sqrt{}$

$h^2 \doteq$ _____

STEP 2: Find the surface area of each triangular face, which are congruent because it is a square-based pyramid. Round your answer to one decimal place.

Surface area of *each* triangular face $= \dfrac{1}{2}bh$

$= \dfrac{1}{2}($____$)($____$)$

$=$ _____

STEP 3: Find the *total* surface area of the pyramid.

Since there are 4 congruent triangular faces:

SA of triangular faces $= 4($_____$)$

$=$ _____

SA of base $=$ _____ $\times$ _____

$=$ _____

The *total* surface area of the pyramid is _____ $+$ _____ $=$ _____.

5. The foundation of a new garage has walls that are 2.5 m high. The garage is 8 m long and 10 m wide. The walls of the foundation are to be sprayed with a waterproofing tar.
   a) Find the surface area of the exterior walls of the garage.

   b) The waterproofing spray costs $13.95 per square metre. How much will the spray cost?

9.3 Surface Area and Volume of Cylinders

Textbook
pp. 381–390

Warm-Up

1. Math Literacy Give two or three different real-life examples of cylinders.	**2. Area of a Circle** Write the formula for the area of a circle. A = _____
3. Radius Where is the radius on a circle? Circle the correct answer. **a)** straight across the centre **b)** around the outside edge **c)** from the centre to the edge	**4. Number Sense** What is the three-digit decimal value of π?
5. Convert Measurements Write each measure using the indicated units. **a)** 315 ft to yards **b)** 0.185 m to millimetres **c)** 22 300 mm^2 to square centimetres **d)** 5184 in.^{3} to cubic feet	**6. Rearrange Formulas** Rearrange each formula to isolate the indicated variable. **a)** $PV = nRT$, for n **b)** $P = 2(l + w)$, for w
7. Algebraic Expressions Find the value of V when $l = 22$ m, $w = 18$ m, and $h = 20$ m. $V = lwh$	**8. Algebraic Equations** Find the value of SA when $l = 5$ in., $w = 2$ in., and $h = 1.5$ in. $SA = 2lw + 2lh + 2wh$

Date: _____

Practise

Where necessary, round your answers to one decimal place. Use $\pi = 3.14$.

1. Find the surface area of the cylinder.

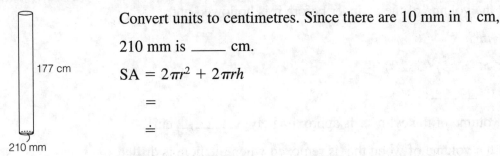

$SA = 2\pi r^2 + 2\pi rh$

$= 2\pi(\underline{\quad})^2 + 2\pi(\underline{\quad})(\underline{\quad})$

$\doteq \underline{\qquad} + \underline{\qquad}$

$\doteq \underline{\qquad}$

The surface area of the cylinder is approximately _____ cm².

2. Find the surface area of the cylinder.

Convert units to centimetres. Since there are 10 mm in 1 cm,

210 mm is ____ cm.

$SA = 2\pi r^2 + 2\pi rh$

$=$

$\doteq$

The surface area of the cylinder is approximately _____ cm².

3. Find the volume of the cylinder.

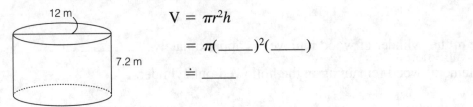

$V = \pi r^2 h$

$= \pi(\underline{\quad})^2(\underline{\quad})$

$\doteq \underline{\quad}$

The volume of the cylinder is approximately _____ m³.

4. Find the volume of the cylinder.

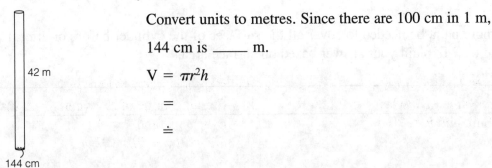

Convert units to metres. Since there are 100 cm in 1 m,

144 cm is ____ m.

$V = \pi r^2 h$

$=$

$\doteq$

The volume of the cylinder is approximately _____ m³.

5. A piece of wood to be used as part of a child's toy has the shape of a cylinder. The cylinder has a height of 18 cm and a radius of 4 cm. The cylinder is hollowed out by drilling a hole with radius 1.5 cm through it lengthwise.

Section 9.3

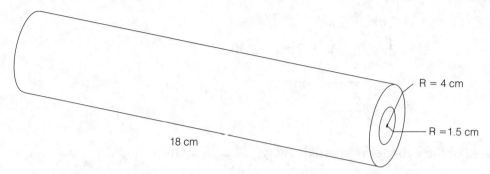

R = 4 cm

R = 1.5 cm

18 cm

a) Find the volume of the cylinder before it is hollowed out.

$V = \pi r^2 h$

$= \pi(\underline{\hspace{1cm}})^2(\underline{\hspace{1cm}})$

$\doteq \underline{\hspace{2cm}}$

The volume of the cylinder is approximately _____ cm^3.

b) Find the volume of wood that is removed when the hole is drilled.

$V = \pi r^2 h$

$= \pi(\underline{\hspace{1cm}})^2(\underline{\hspace{1cm}})$

$\doteq \underline{\hspace{2cm}}$

The volume of the cylinder of wood removed is approximately _____ cm^3.

c) Find the volume of wood remaining in the hollowed-out cylinder.

6. Would more paint be needed to cover all the surfaces of the cylinder before or after it was hollowed out? Explain your answer based on surface area.

_____

_____

9.4 Volume of Cones and Spheres

Textbook
pp. 391–397

Warm-Up

1. Math Literacy	2. Cones
Sydney says that if all of the side lengths of a cube are doubled, the volume of the cube will also double. Is she correct? Explain.	Give two real-life examples of cone-shaped objects.

3. Pythagorean Theorem	4. Spheres
Find the length of side EF to the nearest centimetre. 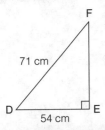	Give two real-life examples of sphere-shaped objects, other than a ball.

5. Convert Measurements	6. Rearrange Formulas
Write each measure using the indicated units. **a)** 42 km to metres **b)** 352 cm to millimetres **c)** 573 cm³ to cubic millimetres **d)** 1250 m² to square feet	Rearrange each formula for the indicated variable. **a)** $P = I^2R$, for I **b)** $D = \dfrac{m}{V}$, for V

7. Algebra	8. Evaluate Expressions
Solve for the unknown values. Use $\pi = 3.14$. **a)** $V = \pi r^2 h$ for $h = 22$ in. and $r = 5$ in. **b)** $SA = 2\pi r^2 + 2\pi rh$ for $r = 16$ cm and $h = 54$ cm	If π equals 3.14, evaluate $\dfrac{1}{3}\pi(2)(5)$. Round your answer to one decimal place.

Practise

Where necessary, round your answers to one decimal place. Use $\pi = 3.14$.

1. Find the volume of each cone. Convert measures to the same units where necessary.

   a)

   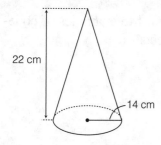

   $$V = \frac{1}{3}\pi r^2 h$$

   $$= \frac{1}{3}\pi(\underline{\quad})^2(\underline{\quad})$$

   $$\doteq \underline{\qquad}$$

   The volume of the cone is approximately _____ cm³.

   b)

   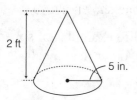

   Convert units to inches. Since there are 12 in. in 1 ft,

   2 ft is _____ in.

   $$V =$$

   $$= \underline{\quad}(\underline{\quad})^2(\underline{\quad})$$

   $$\doteq \underline{\qquad}$$

   The volume of the cone is approximately _____ in³.

2. Find the volume of each sphere.

   a)

   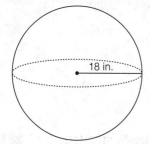

   $$V = \frac{4}{3}\pi r^3$$

   $$= \frac{4}{3}\pi(\underline{\quad})^3$$

   $$\doteq \underline{\qquad}$$

   The volume of the sphere is approximately _____ in.³

   b)

   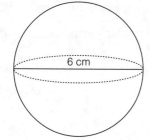

   $$V =$$

   $$= \underline{\quad}(\underline{\quad})^3$$

   $$\doteq \underline{\qquad}$$

   The volume of the sphere is approximately _____ cm³.

Date: _____

3. A cone has radius 18 in. and height 100 in.
   a) Find the volume of the cone.

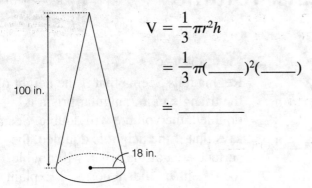

$$V = \frac{1}{3}\pi r^2 h$$

$$= \frac{1}{3}\pi(\rule{1cm}{0.4pt})^2(\rule{1cm}{0.4pt})$$

$$\doteq \rule{2cm}{0.4pt}$$

The volume of the cone is approximately _____ in³.

b) The volume of a particular sphere is half the volume of the cone shown above.
   Find the radius of the sphere.

$$V = \frac{4}{3}\pi r^3$$

Now rearrange the equation to solve for r, knowing the volume of the sphere equals $\frac{1}{2}$ the volume of the cone.

c) What is the diameter of the sphere?

4. A woodworker carves a sphere from a solid cube of wood that has a side length of 18 cm.
   a) What is the radius of the largest sphere the woodworker can carve from the cube?

   b) What is the volume of this sphere?

9.5 Solve Problems Involving Surface Area and Volume

Textbook pp. 398–405

Warm-Up

1. Convert Measurements

Write each measure using the units indicated.

a) 31 yd to feet

b) 0.0042 m to millimetres

c) 2276 cm² to square metres

d) 62 yd³ to cubic feet

2. Math Literacy

Regina tells Seema that if the height of the triangle in a triangular prism is doubled, the volume will double. Seema says that if the height is doubled, the surface area of the prism will double, too. Is either student correct? Explain your answer.

3. Number Sense

A square prism has a height of 8 in. and a base with 6-in. sides. Calculate the area of the base.

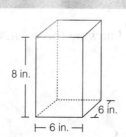

8 in.

6 in.

6 in.

4. Volume

Calculate the volume of the prism in question 3.

5. Rearrange Formulas

Rearrange each formula to isolate the indicated variable.

a) $SA = 2\pi r^2 + 2\pi rh$, for h

b) $E = mc^2$, for c

6. Pythagorean Theorem

Find the value of x.

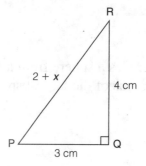

R

2 + x

4 cm

P

3 cm

Q

Practise

Date: _____

Where necessary, round your answers to one decimal place.

1. Find the volume of each shape.

a)

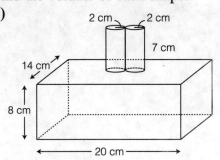

Cylinders:

V =

Rectangular Prism:

V =

b)

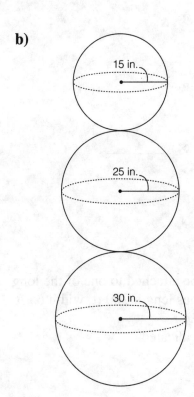

Sphere A

V =

Sphere B

V =

Sphere C

V =

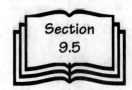

2. All sides, including the bottom, of the birdhouse shown below are to be painted.

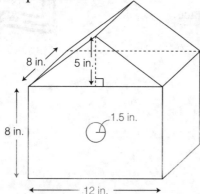

What is the total surface area that will be painted?

Area of back = _____ × _____

            = _____

Area of front = _____ × _____ − _____

            = _____

Area of 2 sides = _____ × _____ × _____

            = _____

Area of base = _____ × _____

            = _____

Area of front and back triangles = _____ × _____ × _____

                             = _____

Area of roof = _____ × _____

            = _____

Total surface area to be painted = _____

3. A warehouse has the shape of a rectangular prism with a cube attached to one of the long sides. The part of the warehouse that is a rectangular prism has length 200 ft, width 65 ft and height 25 ft. The part that is a cube has side length 20 ft.
   a) Make a sketch of the warehouse with the measurements indicated.

   b) What is the total volume of the warehouse?

Chapter 9 Review

9.1 Volume of Prisms and Pyramids, textbook pages 364–371

1. Find the volume of the prism. If necessary, round your answers to one decimal place. Use $\pi = 3.14$.

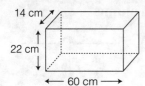

14 cm
22 cm
← 60 cm →

$V = \underline{\hspace{2cm}} \times \underline{\hspace{2cm}} \times \underline{\hspace{2cm}}$

$= \underline{\hspace{2cm}}$

$= \underline{\hspace{2cm}}$

2. Find the volume of the pyramid.

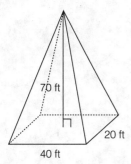

70 ft
20 ft
40 ft

$V = \underline{\hspace{1cm}}$ area of $\underline{\hspace{1cm}} \times \underline{\hspace{2cm}}$

$= \underline{\hspace{2cm}}$

$= \underline{\hspace{2cm}}$

9.2 Surface Area of Prisms and Pyramids, textbook pages 372–380

3. Find the surface area of the prism.

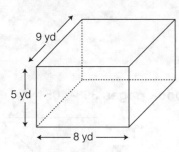

9 yd
5 yd
← 8 yd →

Two faces have dimensions _____ cm by _____ cm.

Area = _____ × _____

= _____

Two faces have dimensions _____ cm by _____ cm.

Area = _____ × _____

= _____

Two faces have dimensions _____ cm by _____ cm.

Area = _____ × _____

= _____

Surface Area = 2(_____) + 2(_____) + 2(_____)

= _____

The surface area of the prism is _____ yd².

9.3 Surface Area and Volume of Cylinders, textbook pages 381–390

Chapter 9
Review

4. Find the surface area and volume of the cylinder.

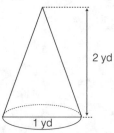

5 in.

14 in.

Circular Top

SA = _____

Side

SA = _____ × _____

Cylinder

SA =

Volume

V = _____ r^2 _____

=

=

5. Find the volume of each object.

a)

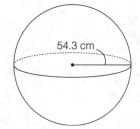

2 yd

1 yd

V = _____ r^2 _____

=

=

b)

54.3 cm

V = _____ r^3

=

=

9.5 Solve Problems Involving Surface Area and Volume, textbook pages 398–405

6. The composite shape shown below is a rectangular prism with a cube removed from one corner.

a) Find the surface area of the composite shape.

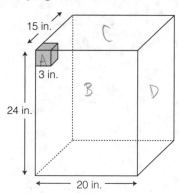

15 in.

C

A

3 in.

B

D

24 in.

20 in.

b) Find the volume of the composite shape.

ANSWERS

Chapter 1 Measurement Systems and Similar Triangles

Get Set

1. a) $\frac{1}{12}, \frac{1}{8}, \frac{1}{4}, \frac{1}{2}$ **b)** $1\frac{1}{2}, 1\frac{3}{4}, \frac{17}{8}, 2\frac{1}{4}, 2\frac{3}{8}$

   c) $\frac{1}{6}, \frac{1}{5}, \frac{1}{3}, \frac{1}{2}$

2. a) $\frac{17}{12}$ **b)** $\frac{1}{4}$ **c)** 81   **d)** $4\frac{1}{4}$

3. a) 1:2   **b)** 3:1   **c)** 6:5   **d)** 2:11

4. a) $m = \frac{3}{2}$ **b)** $y = 1$ **c)** $t = 33$ **d)** $x = 21$

5. a) $a = 125°, b = 55°$ **b)** $a = 95°, b = 85°, c = 95°$
   c) $a = 75°$

1.1: Imperial Measure

Warm-Up

1. a) length   **b)** weight
   c) length   **d)** volume

2. a) 24 in.   **b)** 60 in.

3. 9 ft²

4. a) 15 ft   **b)** 5 ft   **c)** 2 ft

5. Answers may vary.

6. a) 6   **b)** 3

7. a) inches   **b)** fluid ounces   **c)** pounds

8. a) Answers may vary.   **b)** Answers may vary.

Practise

1. 16

2. No, a 1-gal jug can only hold 4 qt.

3. a) 36 in.   **b)** 31 in.   **c)** 102 in.

4. a) 5′11″   **b)** 5′6″   **c)** 18′

5. a) 5.5 lb   **b)** 4200 lb   **c)** 12 lb

6. a) 39 600 sq ft   **b)** $237 600   **c)** $99 000

7. 48 quarts

8. 4 miles

9. 67 in.

10. 6 cups

11. a) 72 sq ft   **b)** $360.00

1.2: Conversions Between Metric and Imperial Systems

Warm-Up

1. Length: millimetre, centimetre, metre, kilometre
Volume: millilitres, litres
Mass: milligrams, grams, kilograms

2. a) 4.2 cm   **b)** 12 000 g   **c)** 180 cm   **d)** 2.4 km   **e)** 0.98 g

3. a) Answers may vary.   **b)** Answers may vary.

4. a) 10 pt   **b)** 48 in.   **c)** 1.5 lbs   **d)** 6 ft   **e)** 12 qt

5. a) centimetres   **b)** grams   **c)** millilitres

6. a) Answers may vary.   **b)** Answers may vary.

7. a) 420 000   **b)** 5.6   **c)** 2.458   **d)** 6.5   **e)** 4.25

8. a) Answers may vary.   **b)** Answers may vary.

Practise

1. a) 74°F   **b)** 136°F   **c)** −18°F

2. a) 29°C   **b)** −25°C   **c)** 96°C

3. a) 4 tbsp   **b)** 5.5 lb   **c)** 30 cm   **d)** 165 mL

4. a) Answers may vary.   **b)** Answers may vary.

5. 8 cups

6. a) 212°F   **b)** 32°F

7. a) 1100 miles   **b)** 1760 km
   c) 3520 km   **d)** 221.76 L

1.3 Similar Triangles

Warm-Up

1. $\angle d, \angle e, \angle h$

2. $\angle a$ and $\angle c$, $\angle b$ and $\angle d$

3. AB = DE = 6 cm
AC = DF = 7.5 cm
BC = EF = 4.5 cm

4. $\angle TSU$ and $\angle RSQ$, $\angle RST$ and $\angle QSU$

5. Answers may vary. Triangles will have equal sides and corresponding angles.

6. $\angle S = 20°$, $\angle X = 105°$

7. a) AB = 4   **b)** LM = 6

8. $\angle MRS = \angle MUV = \angle MKL$;
$\angle MSR = \angle MVU = \angle MLK$

Practise

1. $x = 77°$, $y = 71°$

2. a) JK, KL, JL
   b) Since $\triangle RST \sim \triangle JKL$, then the lengths of the corresponding sides are proportional.
   c) $\frac{RS}{JK} = \frac{ST}{KL}$
     $\frac{RS}{16} = \frac{27}{18}$
     $RS = \frac{16 \times 27}{18}$
     $RS \doteq 24$

3. a) Answers may vary. Yes, the triangles are similar because they have equal corresponding angles.
   b) $\frac{CE}{AB} = \frac{EF}{AF}$
     $\frac{CE}{3.1} = \frac{2.9}{3.8}$
     $CE = \frac{3.1 \times 2.9}{3.8}$
     $CE \doteq 2.4$ cm

4. a)

   b) Answers may vary. Yes triangles ABE and ACD are similar because they have equal corresponding angles.
   c) $x = 20$ m

1.4 Solve Problems Using Similar Triangles

Warm-Up
1. DF and GF, DE and GH, EF and HF
2. **a)** all three pairs of sides. **b)** all three pairs of angles
3. AB = $\dfrac{15 \times 5}{3}$
   AB = 25
4. Answers may vary.
5. The side lengths of Triangle A are five times as long as the side lengths of Triangle B.
6. ∠WXV and ∠YXZ, ∠VWX and ∠XYZ, ∠XVW and ∠XZY
7. **a)** $b = \dfrac{3}{2}$ **b)** $m = 12$
8. MN = 9 cm

Practise
1. **a)** Yes, △ABC and △DEF are similar because they have equal corresponding angles.
   b) Since △ABC ~ △DEF, corresponding angles are equal.
   Therefore, ∠C = ∠F
   $\qquad\qquad = 42°$
   and ∠D = ∠A
   $\qquad\qquad = 34°$

   $\dfrac{BC}{EF} = \dfrac{AB}{DE}$ $\qquad$ $\dfrac{DF}{AC} = \dfrac{DE}{AB}$

   $\dfrac{BC}{2.1} = \dfrac{4.0}{2.6}$ $\qquad$ $\dfrac{DF}{5.1} = \dfrac{2.6}{4.0}$

   $BC = \dfrac{2.1 \times 4.0}{2.6}$ $\qquad$ $DF = \dfrac{5.1 \times 2.6}{4.0}$

   $BC \doteq 3.2$ cm $\qquad$ $DF \doteq 3.3$ cm

2. **a)** Triangle ADE and triangle ACB are similar because they have equal corresponding angles.
   b) $\dfrac{CB}{DE} = \dfrac{AB}{AE}$

   $\dfrac{CB}{40} = \dfrac{102}{32}$

   $CB = \dfrac{40 \times 102}{32}$

   $CB \doteq 127.5$ m

3. **a)** Yes, triangle ABC and triangle DEF are similar because they have equal corresponding angles.
   b) DF = 294
   c) $\dfrac{EF}{BC} = \dfrac{DF}{AC}$

   $\dfrac{EF}{2} = \dfrac{294}{4}$

   $EF = \dfrac{2 \times 294}{4}$

   $EF = 147$ m

Chapter 1 Review

1. Answers may vary.
2. **a)** 17.6 lbs **b)** 480 fl oz **c)** 57.2°C
   d) 13.3 L **e)** 11.0 m **f)** 1545 ft
3. **a)** 63.6 kg **b)** 2035 mg
4. **a)** $2.99 U.S./gal
   b) Port Huron offers a better price for gas.
5. $x = 3.8$ cm, $y = 4.4$ cm
6. **a)** 450 m

b) △DRC and △ERB are similar because the corresponding angles are equal.
c) 40 m
7. 12.6 m

Chapter 2 Right Triangle Trigonometry
Get Set

Solving Proportions
1. **a)** $x = 7$ **b)** $y = 33$ **c)** $z = 36$ **d)** $x = 3$
2. **a)** $x = 3.143$ **b)** $y = 67.5$ **c)** $x = 7.125$ **d)** $t = 32.5$
3. **a)** 14° **b)** 11° **c)** 32 **d)** 83°
4. **a)** 22.4 **b)** 163.7 **c)** 2.4 **d)** 0.8
5. **a)** 0.148 3 **b)** 27.005 2 **c)** 45.760 3
   d) 3.421 8 **e)** 15.763 2 **f)** 109.524 7

2.1 The Pythagorean Theorem

Warm-Up
1. **a)** 11.1 **b)** 8.2 **c)** 3.5 **d)** 17.3
2. isosceles
3. **a)** 15 **b)** 13
4. Answers may vary.
5. obtuse isosceles triangle
6. right, hypotenuse, legs
7. **a)** 3 **b)** 6
8. scalene right triangle

Practise: The Pythagorean Theorem
1. **a)** 5 **b)** 18.6 cm **c)** 26.2 **d)** 20.2 in.
2. **a)** 17.3 m **b)** 11.3 **c)** 17.2 ft **d)** 8.2
3. Simone is incorrect since the Pythagorean theorem can only be applied to right triangles and the triangle on the right is not.
4. Step 1: Find the difference between the square of the hypotenuse and square of the given leg.
   Step 2: x is equal to the square root of answer found in Step 1.
5. 39.7 cm
6. **a)** 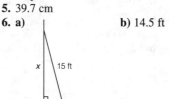 **b)** 14.5 ft

2.2 Explore Ratio and Proportion in Right Triangles

Warm-Up
1. **a)** 0.4 **b)** 2.4 **c)** 0.875 **d)** 1.25
2. **a)** $\dfrac{4}{9}$ **b)** $\dfrac{1}{4}$ **c)** $\dfrac{1}{8}$ **d)** $\dfrac{2}{5}$
3. Answers may vary.
4. **a)** 3:2 **b)** 3:4 **c)** 1:4 **d)** 3:7
5. **a)** 11 **b)** 8 **c)** 10 **d)** 20
6. Answers may vary.
7. $x = 48°$
8. $x = 45°$; $y = 45°$

Practise: Explore Ratio and Proportion in Right Triangles
1. **a)** DE = adjacent side
   b) DE would become the opposite side and EF would become the adjacent side.

2. a) 0.71   **b)** 0.54   **c)** 0.5

3. a)

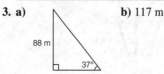

b) 8.34   **c)** 0.120   **d)** the slope

4. a) 12 cm   **b)** 0.92, 0.38

2.3 The Sine and Cosine Ratios

Warm-Up

1. adjacent = QR, hypotenuse = QS
2. 2:4.5; 0.44
3. An adjacent side is a leg of a right triangle adjacent to a given angle.
4. 7:7.6; 0.92
5. Answers may vary.
6. Answers may vary.
7. 7:5, 1.4
8. Adjacent = ZX, hypotenuse = ZY

Practise: The Sine and Cosine Ratios

1. a) 0.2588   **b)** 0.2079   **c)** 0.7986
    d) 0.9903   **e)** 0.9135   **f)** 0.1564

2. a) 9°   **b)** 70°   **c)** 77°
    d) 54°   **e)** 27°   **f)** 46°

3. a) 46 cm   **b)** 27 cm   **c)** 17 cm   **d)** 181 cm

4. 21.3 m

5. a) 27.9 m   **b)** 8.7 m

2.4 The Tangent Ratio

Warm-Up

1. opposite, hypotenuse
2. $\sin 25° = \dfrac{y}{12}$
   $12 \sin 25° = y$
   $y = 5.1$ cm
3. $\sin 42° = \dfrac{m}{47}$
4. adjacent; hypotenuse
5. sine
6. $\cos 30° = \dfrac{j}{19}$
   $19 \cos 30° = j$
   $j = 16.5$ cm
7. $r = 18.1$ cm
8. $\cos 32° = \dfrac{p}{51}$

Practise: The Tangent Ratio

1. a) 0.4122   **b)** 3.7321   **c)** 0.2126   **d)** 1.0000
2. a) 33°   **b)** 70°   **c)** 48°   **d)** 19°
3. 20 cm, 21 cm, 20, 21, 44°
4. a) $\dfrac{8}{5}$ **b)** $\dfrac{17}{21}$ **c)** $\dfrac{6}{31}$
5. Jeremy forgot to check if triangle ABC is a right triangle. Since triangle ABC is not a right triangle, Jeremy cannot use the Pythagorean theorem.
6. a) 14°   **b)** 14°
    c) The measure of angle Z is the same for parts (a) and (b). This is because both ladders are placed with a 4:1 ratio.

2.5 Solve Problems Using Right Triangles

Warm-Up

1. $\tan 32° = \dfrac{u}{25}$
2. $e = 6.9$ cm
3. 47 cm
4. No, the tangent ratio does not involve the hypotenuse.
5. 15 m
6. Answers may vary.
7. $\tan 37° = \dfrac{12}{d}$
   $d\tan 37° = 12$
   $d = \dfrac{12}{\tan 37°}$
   $d = 15.9$ cm
8. both

Practise: Solve Problems Using Right Triangles

1. a) 19.0 ft   **b)** angle of depression

2.

Distance From Object (m)	Angle of Elevation (°)	Height From Transit to Top of Object (m)	Height of Object (m)
8.5	48.2	9.5	10.7
9.3	44.2	9.0	10.2
15.8	51.3	19.7	20.9
7.3	49.6	8.6	9.8

3. a)

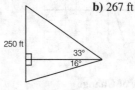

    b) 117 m

4. a) 172.8 ft   **b)** 40°

5. a)

250 ft   33°   16°

    b) 267 ft

Chapter 2 Review

1. 17.0 cm
2. KM = hypotenuse, KL = adjacent side, LM = opposite side
   a) $\dfrac{LM}{KL}$ **b)** $\dfrac{KL}{KM}$ **c)** $\dfrac{LM}{KM}$
3. 38.7°
4. a)

18 ft   20°

    b) 52.6 ft

5. a)

25°   77°   x   y   77°   50 m

    b) 239.9 m

Chapter 3 Linear Relations

Get Set

1. a) 4   **b)** 15   **c)** 11

2. a) $\dfrac{1}{2}$ **b)** $\dfrac{1}{5}$ **c)** $\dfrac{1}{4}$ **d)** $\dfrac{3}{5}$

3. a) -13 **b)** -5 **c)** $\dfrac{1}{16}$

4. $A(2, 3)$, $B(-6, 5)$, $C(-5, -2)$, $D(-6, 0)$, $E(5, -5)$

5. a) 3   **b)** 3   **c)** -4

6. a) -4 **b)** 11   **c)** -59

3.1 Slope as a Rate of Change

Warm-Up

1. a) $\dfrac{2}{3}$ **b)** $\dfrac{2}{5}$ **c)** $\dfrac{4}{7}$ **d)** $\dfrac{1}{2}$

2. a) 8   **b)** -13 **c)** -1 **d)** 2

3.

x	y
0	5
1	7
2	9
3	11
4	13

4. $63

5.

x	y
-2	-2
-1	1
0	4
1	7
2	10

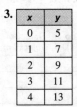

$y = 3x + 4$

6. Answers may vary.

Practise: Slope as a Rate of Change

1. a) $y = -2x + 2$

x	y	Rate of Change
-2	6	
-1	4	-2
0	2	-2
1	0	-2
2	-2	-2

b) $y = 5x - 1$

x	y	Rate of Change
-2	-11	
-1	-6	5
0	-1	5
1	4	5
2	9	5

2. a)

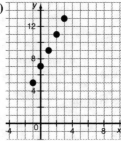

b) The rate of change is 2.

3. a)

Hours Worked	Total Earnings ($)	Rate of Change
0	0	
1	8.25	8.25
2	16.50	8.25
3	24.75	8.25
4	33.00	8.25
5	41.25	8.25
6	49.50	8.25

b) $8.25/h

c)

d) Answers may vary.

e) slope $= 8.25$

f) The rate of change is $8.25/h. This represents the money Lewis earns per hour.

4. a)

x	y
-2	-2
-1	0
0	2
1	4
2	6
3	8

b)

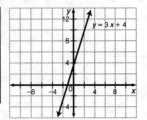

c) Answers may vary.

d) slope $= 2$

5. a)

Hours Worked	Number of Dolls Packed	Rate of Change
0	0	
1	15	15
2	30	15
3	45	15
4	60	15
5	75	15
6	90	15

b) 15 dolls per hour

c) The rate of change represents the speed that Amy packs dolls.

3.2 Investigate Slope and *y*-Intercept Using Technology

Warm-Up

1. slope

2. a) -13　　**b)** -8　　**c)** 11　　**d)** 3

3. a) $\dfrac{3}{-9} = -\dfrac{1}{3}$　　**b)** $\dfrac{-4}{-12} = \dfrac{1}{3}$

4. \$6.50/h

5. $\dfrac{18 - 12}{4 - 1} = 2$

6. Change in price from changing in toppings.

Practise: Investigate Slope and *y*-Intercept Using Technology

1. a) slope: 2, *y*-intercept: 0

b) slope: 4, *y*-intercept: -5

c) slope: -1, *y*-intercept: 6

d) slope: $-\dfrac{1}{2}$, *y*-intercept: $\dfrac{5}{2}$

2. a) $y = \dfrac{7}{2}x + 9$　　**b)** $y = -3x + 3$

c) $y = -3$　　**d)** $y = 7x$

3. a) slope: -3, *y*-intercept: 8, equation: $y = -3x + 8$

b) slope: 2, *y*-intercept: -3, equation: $y = 2x - 3$

c) slope: 1, *y*-intercept: 2, equation: $y = x + 2$

4. a) Answers may vary.

b) Change the window settings.

c) slope　　**d)** *y*-intercept　　**e)** \$10 000

3.3 Properties of Slopes of Lines

Warm-Up

1. $p = \dfrac{\text{rise}}{\text{run}} = \dfrac{30}{40} = \dfrac{3}{4}$

2. $m = \dfrac{2}{5}$

3. Answers may vary.

4. a) -3　　**b)** $\dfrac{4}{9}$　　**c)** $-\dfrac{3}{2}$　　**d)** 3

5. $f = \dfrac{\text{rise}}{\text{run}} = \dfrac{30}{70} = \dfrac{3}{7}$

6. $m = \dfrac{\text{rise}}{\text{run}} = \dfrac{8}{2} = 4$

Practise: Properties of Slopes of Lines

1. a) i) 3　　**ii)** 0　　**iii)** $-\dfrac{1}{2}$　　**iv)** 1

v) -1　　**vi)** 0　　**vii)** $\dfrac{1}{3}$

b)

Positive Slope	Negative Slope	Zero Slope
$y = 3x + 4$	$y = -\dfrac{1}{2}x + 5$	$y = 4$
$y = x - 2$	$y = -x - 5$	$y = -1$
$y = \dfrac{1}{3}x + 5$		

2. a) Answers may vary. The equation must have a slope of 4.

b) Answers may vary. The equation must have a slope less than -1.

c) Answers may vary. The equation must have a slope of less than 3.

d) Answers may vary. The equation must have a slope of $-\dfrac{1}{2}$.

3. a) $y = -2x - 4$　　**b)** $y = x + 4$

c) $y = -\dfrac{4}{3}x - 6$　　**d)** $y = -\dfrac{3}{2}x$

4. $s = \dfrac{\text{rise}}{\text{run}} = \dfrac{3}{7}$; The slope of the ramp is $\dfrac{3}{7}$.

5. $w = \dfrac{\text{rise}}{\text{run}} = \dfrac{481}{377} = \dfrac{37}{29}$; The slope of the ramp is $\dfrac{37}{29}$.

3.4 Determine the Equation of a Line

Warm-Up

1. $m = \dfrac{\text{rise}}{\text{run}} = -\dfrac{5}{4}$; *y*-intercept: 8

2. $m = \dfrac{\text{rise}}{\text{run}} = \dfrac{4}{2} = 2$; *y*-intercept: -1

3.

x	*y*	Rate of Change
0	5	
1	2	3
2	-1	3
3	-4	3
4	-7	3

4.

x	*y*	Rate of Change
0	-3	
1	$-\dfrac{5}{2}$	$\dfrac{1}{2}$
2	-2	$\dfrac{1}{2}$
3	$-\dfrac{3}{2}$	$\dfrac{1}{2}$
4	-1	$\dfrac{1}{2}$

5. The *y*-intercept for this relation is 4.

6. The line in question 3 has a negative slope.

Practise: Determine the Equation of a Line

1. a) slope: $\frac{1}{2}$, y-intercept: -9, equation: $y = \frac{1}{2}x - 9$

b) slope: 3, y-intercept: 5, equation: $y = 3x + 5$

c) slope: 0, y-intercept: 5, equation: $y = 5$

2. a) $y = -\frac{1}{3}x + 2$

b) $y = 4x - 3$

c) $y = 3x + 8$

d) $y = -3$

3. a) $y = -2x$

b) $y = \frac{1}{3}x - 4$

c) $y = -4x + 24$

d) $y = \frac{1}{2}x + 7$

4. $y = -3x + 15$

5. a)

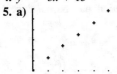

b) $y = \frac{113}{50}x + 412$

c) 412. This represents the mass of the empty beaker.

d) $\frac{113}{50}$

3.5 Graph Linear Relations by Hand

Warm-Up

1. a) $y = 7$

b) $y = 2$

2. The steepest slope is part a) $y = -2x + 1$.

3. No; $y = \frac{2}{3}(3) - 1 = 1 \neq -1$

4. slope: 2

y-intercept: 4

5. slope: 3

y-intercept: -1

6. Slope is the coefficient of the x term. The y-intercept can be determined by substituting in $x = 0$ to get the y-value.

Practise: Graph Linear Relations by Hand

1. a) slope: $-\frac{1}{4}$; y-intercept: 11

b) slope: 5; y-intercept: -9

c) slope: $\frac{4}{5}$; y-intercept: 0

d) slope: -3; y-intercept: $\frac{9}{2}$

2.

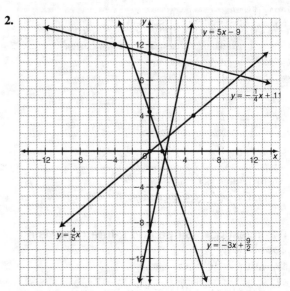

3.

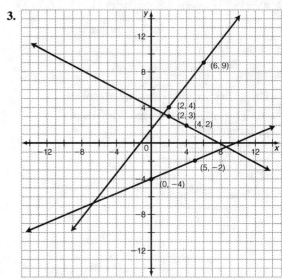

4. a)

Time (s)	0	1	2	3	4
Distance (m)	0	33	66	99	132

b)

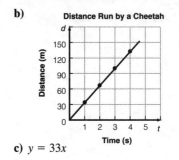

Distance Run by a Cheetah

c) $y = 33x$

5. a)

Distance (km)	0	1	2	3	4
Funds Raised ($)	0	15	30	45	60

b)

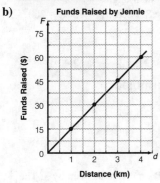

Funds Raised by Jennie

c) $y = 15x$

Chapter 3 Review

1. a)

x	y	Rate of Change
−1	9	
0	6	−3
1	3	−3
2	0	−3
3	−3	−3
4	−6	−3

b)

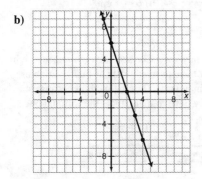

c) −3

2. a)

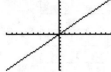

b)

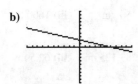

3. a) Answers may vary. The equation must have a slope of 6.

b) Answers may vary. The equation must have a slope of −2.

c) Answers may vary. The equation must have a slope of $\frac{1}{2}$.

4. a) $y = 3x − 1$ **b)** $y = −2x + 3$

c) $y = 4$ **d)** $y = 2.5x − 1$

5. a) $y = −6x + 13$ **b)** $y = \frac{1}{2}x + 8$

c) $y = −\frac{1}{3}x$ **d)** $y = \frac{5}{8}x − 4$

6. a)

Year	0	1	2	3	4
Value of Card ($)	23	35	47	59	71

b)

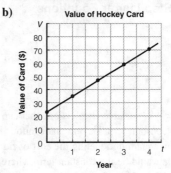

Value of Hockey Card

c) $y = 12t + 23$ **d)** $71.00

Chapter 4 Linear Equations

Get Set

1. a) 60   **b)** 12   **c)** 16   **d)** 110

2. a) $\frac{7}{12}$ **b)** $\frac{1}{20}$ **c)** $\frac{1}{5}$ **d)** $\frac{8}{15}$

3. a) 2   **b)** 8   **c)** 2   **d)** 10

4. a) $4x$ **b)** $7x − 8y$ **c)** $3x − 5y + 3$ **d)** $4k$

5. a) $8y − 12$ **b)** $−2x + 14y$ **c)** $−4x + 32$ **d)** $2y + 2$

6. a) 12   **b)** 44   **c)** 36   **d)** 8

4.1 Solve One- and Two-Step Linear Equations

Warm-Up

1. $\frac{22}{15}$ or $1\frac{7}{15}$

2. x

3. 4

4. First, subtract the value of the y-coordinate of the first point from the value of the y-coordinate of the second point. Second, subtract the value of the x-coordinate of the first point from the value of the x-coordinate of the second point. Then, divide the difference between the y-coordinates by the difference between the x-coordinates. The quotient is the slope.

5. −2

6. $x = 8$

7. $x = 16$

8. $x = 5$

Practise: Solve One- and Two-Step Linear Equations
1. a) $x = -7$ **b)** $x = 2$ **c)** $x = 11$ **d)** $x = 12$
2. a) $x = 5$ **b)** $t = 4$ **c)** $y = 8$ **d)** $k = 8$
3. Answers will vary.
4. a) $k = 9$ **b)** $t = 15$ **c)** $y = 18$ **d)** $x = -10$
5. Answers will vary.
6. a) $x = 4$ **b)** $x = 2$ **c)** $x = 8$ **d)** $x = 25$
e) $x = -\dfrac{7}{3}$ or $-2\dfrac{1}{3}$
f) $x = 22$
7. Substitute $x = 3$; LS $= 4(3) - 7 = 5 =$ RS.
8. a) 72 cm^2 **b)** 48 in.
9. a) $C = 125n$ **b)** \$5 250   **c)** No
d) \$840 more is needed.

4.2 Solve Multi-Step Linear Equations
Warm-Up
1. $\dfrac{3}{10}$
2. $m = 2$
3. $\dfrac{2}{3}$
4. Answers may vary. A "variable term" is one that can change where a "constant term" is one that cannot. For example, in an equation modeling the cost of riding a taxi, the flat rate would be the constant term where the duration of the ride would be the variable term.
5. 1
6.

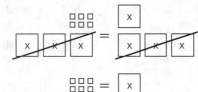

7. $x = 3$
8. $x = -1$

Practise: Solve Multi-Step Linear Equations
1. a) Multiply by 5, add 2, divide by 6.
b) Divide by $\dfrac{2}{5}$, subtract 1.
c) Divide by 4, add 1, divide by 2.
d) Multiply by 3, subtract 1, divide by 22.
2. a) $x = 2$ **b)** $k = 4$
c) $a = \dfrac{5}{2}$ or $2\dfrac{1}{2}$ **d)** $t = 2$
3. a) $d = 8$ **b)** $x = -7$
c) $t = -3$ **d)** $p = 1$
4. Both are correct. The two equations are equivalent.
5. a) $k = 3$ **b)** $x = 13$
c) $y = -60$ **d)** $t = 1$

6. a) $x = 7$ **b)** $k = 5$
7. a) $\angle A = 30°$, $\angle B = 60°$, $\angle C = 90°$
b) $\triangle ABC$ is a scalene triangle.
8. a) Edge Sky Diving Services: $y = 130x + 200$
JerrMo: $y = 145x$
b) JerrMo
9. a) 8 weeks   **b)** \$150   **c)** 3 weeks

4.3 Model With Formulas
Warm-Up
1. $\dfrac{11}{18}$
2. $x = 14$
3. $x = 3$
4. First, add 1 to 20. Then divide the sum by 3. The quotient is the solution.
5. $l = 14$
6. 59 km/h
7. 6 years
8. $h = \dfrac{SA - 2l^2}{4l}$

Practise: Model with Formulas
1. a) $t = \dfrac{I}{Pr}$ **b)** $V = \dfrac{nRT}{P}$
c) $a = \dfrac{2(d - vt)}{t^2}$ **d)** $m = \dfrac{(y - b)}{x}$
2. a) $b = \dfrac{2A - ah}{h}$ **b)** $b = 1$ cm
c) $28 = \dfrac{1}{2}(6 + b)8$
d) Answers may vary. The second method because he would not have to manipulate as many variables.
e) Answers may vary. The first method because she would only have to manipulate the formula once.
3. a) $v = \dfrac{d}{t}$ **b)** $t = \dfrac{d}{v}$
c)

distance (m)	time (s)	velocity (m/s)
4	3	$\dfrac{4}{3}$
6	3	2
75	5	15
28	7	4
121	11	11
85	5	17

4. a) $C = 11f + 18m + 14p + 200$
b) \$703
5. a) i) 60.8 km   **ii)** 360 km   **iii)** 1600 km
b) $M = \dfrac{K}{1.6}$
c) i) 15.625 mi   **ii)** 283.125 mi   **iii)** 62.5 mi
d) 88 km/h
6. a) 75 km/h
b) It would take about 7.33 h.
7. 6.25%

4.4 Convert Linear Equations From Standard Form

Warm-Up
1. 24
2. $x = 20$
3. $x = 5$
4. **a)** slope   **b)** standard form
5. $y = -4x + 7$
6. $y = 3x + 4$
7. slope: $\dfrac{3}{4}$, y-intercept: -2
8. slope: $\dfrac{1}{3}$, y-intercept: -4

Practise: Convert Linear Equations From Standard Form
1. **a)** Subtract y, multiply by -1.
   b) Add $4y$, divide by 4.
   c) Subtract $5y$, divide by -5.
   d) Add $2y$, divide by 2.
2. **a)** $y = -3x + 5$; slope: -3, y-intercept: 5
   b) $y = x$; slope: 1, y-intercept: 0
   c) $y = 4$; slope: 0, y-intercept: 4
   d) $y = \dfrac{2}{5}x + 3$; slope: $\dfrac{2}{5}$, y-intercept: 3
4. $C = -37$
5. $A = 2$
6. $m = 4$
7. **a)** $C = 42n + 2000$ **b)** \$12 500
8. **a)** $C = 44n + 2500$ **b)** \$13 500
   c) Chisholm Hall costs \$1000 more.

Chapter 4 Review

2. **a)** $x = 19$ **b)** $t = 7$ **c)** $h = 4$ **d)** $b = 6$
3. **a)** $x = 5$ **b)** $t = 12$ **c)** $k = -1$ **d)** $x = 20$
4. **a)** $t = 3$ **b)** $x = 7$ **c)** $x = 14$ **d)** $y = 10$
   e) $x = -\dfrac{17}{14}$ or $-1\dfrac{3}{14}$ **f)** $k = 0$
5. **a)** $P = \dfrac{I}{rt}$ **b)** $r = \dfrac{I}{Pt}$ **c)** $t = \dfrac{I}{Pr}$

6.

interest (\$)	principal (\$)	rate (%)	time (years)
500	2000	**6.25%**	4
66	600	5.5%	2
120	1200	4%	**2.5**
450	**1000**	5%	9

7. **a)** $y = -\dfrac{1}{4}x + 4$; slope: $-\dfrac{1}{4}$, y-intercept: 4
   b) $y = \dfrac{3}{2}x + 5$; slope: $\dfrac{3}{2}$, y-intercept: 5
   c) $y = -\dfrac{8}{5}x + 3$; slope: $-\dfrac{8}{5}$, y-intercept: 3
   d) $y = -3x$; slope: -3, y-intercept: 0
8. **a)** $b = -5$ **b)** $b = -22$ **c)** $b = -31$ **d)** $b = 15$

Chapter 5: Linear Systems

Get Set
1. **a)** $2c + 5$ **b)** $-3x - 9$ **c)** $-y + 10$
2. **a)** $x = 3y + 7$ **b)** $x = 3y + 4$
   c) $x = -\dfrac{4}{3}y + 6$ **d)** $x = 2y - \dfrac{5}{2}$
3. **a)** $x = 14$ **b)** $x = 1$ **c)** $x = 3$
4. slope: 3, y-intercept: -4,

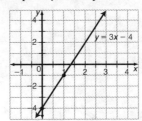

5. **a)** Answers may vary. Let l be Leah's age and j be Joan's age. $l + j = 29$
   b) Let h be the number of hours the equipment was rented and C be the total cost including the flat fee. $C = 10h + 25$

5.1 Solve Linear Systems by Graphing

Warm-Up
1. **a)** $\dfrac{5}{2}$ **b)** -2 **c)** $-\dfrac{10}{2} + \dfrac{6}{2}$
2. **a)** $y = -2x + 7$ **b)** $y = -2x - 4$
3. **a)** Answers may vary, however, the graph should be a straight line.
   b) It would represent the y-intercept.
4. **a)** $y = 5$ **b)** $y = -6$ **c)** $y = 3$
5. It will have travelled 132 m.
6. $y = 2x + 5$

Practise: Solve Linear Systems by Graphing
1. Answers may vary.
2. **a)** (1) $y = 2x + 1$. Slope: 2, y-intercept: 1
        (2) $y = -x + 4$. Slope: -1, y-intercept: 4
   b)

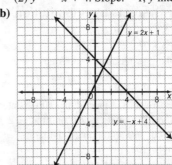

   c) (1, 3)

d) Equation ①
$$LS = -2x \qquad RS = -y + 1$$
$$= -2(1) \qquad = -3 + 1$$
$$= -2 \qquad = -2$$
Equation ②
$$LS = x \qquad RS = -y + 4$$
$$= 1 \qquad = -3 + 4$$
$$= 1$$

e) $(1, 3)$

3. a) Answers
may vary.

b) $(5, 250)$

4. a)

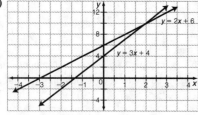

b) $(2, 10)$

c) Equation ①
$$LS = y \qquad RS = 3x + 4$$
$$= 10 \qquad = 3(2) + 4$$
$$= 10$$
Equation ②
$$LS = y \qquad RS = 2x + 6$$
$$= 10 \qquad = 2(2) + 6$$
$$= 10$$

5. a) $y = 25x + 300$

b) $y = 20x + 400$

c) The point of intersection is $(20, 800)$.
This means that if 20 rounds of golf are played, the
cost of joining the women's league costs the same for
both memberships. The cost is $800.

5.2 Solve Linear Systems by Substitution

Warm-Up

1. a) 0   **b)** -9

2. a) y because isolating y requires fewer steps.

  b) x because isolating x requires fewer steps.

3. a) $y = -2x + 4$ **b)** -2 **c)** 4

4. Answers may vary. You can use a grid: mark the y-intercept
at -3, rise 1 and run 4 to mark a next point at $(-2, 4)$
and so on, or you can use a graphing calculator.

5. Celia earns about $76.08.

6.

x	y
−2	7
−1	6
0	5
1	4
2	3

Practise: Solve Linear Systems by Substitution

1. The name is used because you are substituting one
equation into the other to find a solution.

2. a) ② $2x + 1 = 3x - 13$

  b) $2x - 3x = -13 - 1$
$$-1x = -14$$
$$x = 14$$

  c) $y = 2(14) + 1$
$$y = 28 + 1$$
$$y = 29$$

  d) $LS = y \qquad\qquad RS = 3x - 13$
$$= 29 \qquad\qquad = 3(14) - 13$$
$$= 42 - 13$$
$$= 29$$

Yes.
The solution to this linear system is $(14, 29)$.

3. a) $\left(-\dfrac{4}{3}, \dfrac{5}{3}\right)$ **b)** $(8, 3)$

4. a) First hall: $y = 14x + 1000$
Second hall: $y = 16x + 800$

  b) i) $x = 100$ **ii)** $y = 2400$ **iv)** $(100, 2400)$

  c) The solution represents the number of people for
which the cost of renting both halls will be the same.

  d) Dianne should choose the first hall since it only costs
$3100 where the second hall costs $3200.

5.3 Solve Linear Systems by Elimination

Warm-Up

1. a) 12

  b) 22

2. a) $19x + 22$

  b) $6x + 34$

3. Answers may vary. No, it is not a solution to the linear
system, because $(0, 2)$ does not satisfy the first equation.

4. When the *profit* is equal to the *revenue*.

5. a) $9

  b) $1.20

6. $x = \dfrac{3}{5}y + 2$

Practise: Solve Linear Systems by Elimination

1. Answers may vary. It is because addition or subtraction
of equations is used to eliminate one variable.

2. a) $4y = 8$

  b) $y = 2$

  c) $x = 3$

  d) $LS = -2x + 3y \qquad RS = 0$
$$= -2(3) + 3(2)$$
$$= -6 + 6$$
$$= 0$$
The solution to this system is $(3, 2)$.

3. a) 2; x; subtracted; $8x + 34y = 50$

  b) $45y = 45$

  c) $y = 1$

  d) $x = 2$

  e) $LS = -4x + 17y \qquad RS = 25$
$$= -4(2) + 17(1)$$
$$= 8 + 17$$
$$= 25$$
The solution to this system is $(2, 1)$.

4. a) Multiply equation ① by two, then add the two equations.

  b) Subtract equation ② from equation 1.

5.4 Solve Problems Involving Linear Systems

Warm-Up

1. a) 21
   b) 0.8
2. a) $4y = 14$
   b) $5x = 29$
3. Answers may vary. No, since the first difference is not constant.
4. Answers may vary.
5. $119 000
6. $(1, 7)$

Practise: Solve Problems Involving Linear Systems

1. $(1, -5)$
2. a) $5x = 5$
   b) $x = 1$
   c) $y = -5$
   d) LS $= 3x - y$ RS $= 8$
       $= 3(1) - (-5)$
       $= 3 + 5$
       $= 8$
   The solution to this linear equation is $(1, -5)$
3. a) $x + y = 19$
   b) $2x + y = 34$
   c) $x = 15; y = 4$
   d) Answers may vary.
4. a) $C_{Tony} = 5w + 50; C_{Mike} = 10w$
   b) $(10, 100)$
   c) Answers may vary.
   d) For a 10-week contract, both Mike and Tony charge the same amount, $100.
5. $6d + 480k = 361.50$ ①; $2d + 300k = 173.00$ ②;
   $(30.25, 0.375)$

Chapter 5 Review

1. a) Yes, because it satisfies both equations.
   b) No, because it does not satisfy the second equation.
2. a)

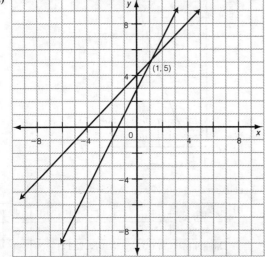

(1, 5)

b)

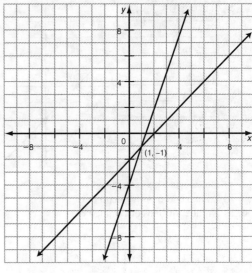

(1, -1)

3. a) $(13, -1)$
   b) $(5, 40)$
   c) Answers may vary. When the solution is not an integer, it is difficult to find the exact solution by graphing by hand.
4. a) $y = x + 4$
   b) $y = \dfrac{2x - 5}{3}$
   c) $y = -3x + 5$
5. a) The total revenue from selling the sweatshirts
   b) $C = 10x + 250$
   c) $R = 20x$
   d) $x = 25; C = R = 500$
   e) $(25, 500)$; 25 sweatshirts
6. a) Answers may vary. Subtract the second equation from the first equation.
   b) Multiply the second equation by 2, then add the resulting equation ③ to equation ①.
7. $(-2, -3)$; substitution, because equation ① already has the variable y isolated.

Chapter 6: Quadratic Relations

Get Set

1. a) 20   **b)** 82
2. a)

x	$y = 3x - 5$
-3	-14
-2	-11
-1	-8
0	-5
1	-2
2	1
3	4

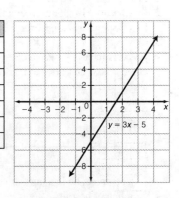

$y = 3x - 5$

b)

x	y = -x - 2
-3	1
-2	0
-1	-1
0	-2
1	-3
2	-4
3	-5

3. a) *x*-intercept: 4, *y*-intercept: 4
b) *x*-intercept: 6, *y*-intercept: −12
4. a) Number of lines of symmetry: 1

b) Number of lines of symmetry: 6

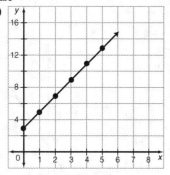

6.1 Explore Non-Linear Relations

Warm-Up

1. A parabola is a quadratic non-linear graph.
2. Linear relation — line of best fit
Non-linear relation — curve of best fit
3. a) 2   **b)** 18
4. Length: 5 cm, Width: 2 cm, Area = 5 × 2
$$= 10 \text{ cm}^2$$
5. Perimeter = 2 × (5 + 12)
$$= 34 \text{ m}$$
6. a) 48   **b)** 45
7. One type of non-linear relation is a quadratic.
8. A graph of a quadratic relation is called a parabola

Practise

1. a)

The points lie in a line, so I drew a line of best fit.

b)

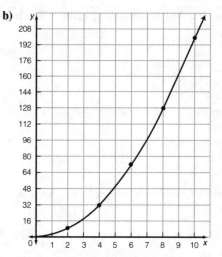

The points do not lie in a line, so I drew a curve of best fit.

2. a)

Side Length (cm)	Surface Area (cm²)
1	6
2	24
3	54
4	96
5	150
6	216

b)

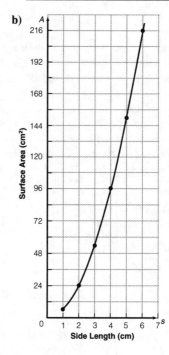

3. a) $P = 2(l + w), A = l \times w$

b)

Length (m)	14	13	12	11	10	9	8
Width (m)	1	2	3	4	5	6	7
Area (m²)	14	26	36	44	50	54	56

c)

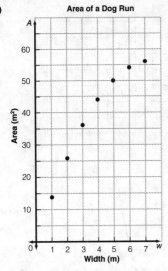

Area of a Dog Run

d) The relation between width and area is non-linear because the points lie on a curve.

4.

Figure	Base	Height	Area
1	2	2	3
2	3	3	6
3	4	4	10
4	5	5	15
5	6	6	21
6	7	7	28

6.2 Model Quadratic Relations

Warm-Up

1. A quadratic relation can be modelled by an equation in the form of $y = ax^2 + bx + c$. It can never be zero.
2. a, b, and c are all quadratic
3. They would form a curve of best fit.
4.

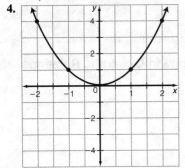

5. **a)** $y = 3x - 2$ **b)** $y = 4x + 5$
6. **a)** $y = 14$ **b)** $y = 8$
7. $y = 3$
8. **a)** 102.6   **b)** 25.1   **c)** 4.2

Practise

1. An equation for a quadratic relation has an x^2-term.
2. It represents a quadratic relation because it has an x^2-term.

3. a)

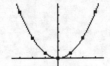

b) A quadratic relation

4. a)

x	y
−5	20
−4	11
−3	4
−2	−1
−1	−4
0	−5
1	−4
2	−1
3	4
4	11
5	20

b) $y = x^2 - 5$
c) A quadratic relation fits the data.

5. **b)** The data appear on the graph in the shape of a parabola, therefore, the data form a quadratic relation.
   c) The equation of the relation is $y = -4.9x^2 + 29.4x$.

6. a)

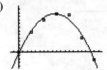

b) The equation of the quadratic relation is
$y = -0.744x^2 + 12.846x - 2.002$.

6.3 Key Features of Quadratic Relations

Warm-Up

1. $y = 4x^2 + 17$
2.

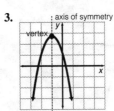

3.

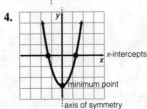

4.

5.

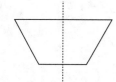

6.

7. $y = 28$

8. $y = -x^2 - \dfrac{2}{3}x + 2$. If $x = 3$, $y = -9$

Practise

1. a)

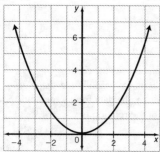

b)

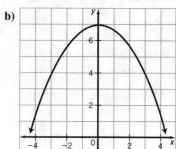

c)

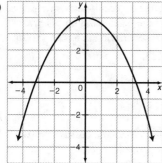

2.

x	$y = x^2$
−3	9
−2	4
−1	1
0	0
1	1
2	4
3	9

x	$y = 2x^2$
−3	18
−2	8
−1	2
0	0
1	2
2	8
3	18

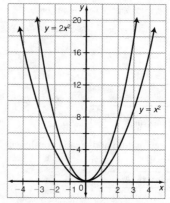

3. a) Similarities: same vertex, same axis of symmetry, both open upward

Differences: the parabola $y = 2x^2$ is narrower than the parabola $y = x^2$

b) The reason for the difference is the coefficient of 2 for x^2.

c) Changing the sign of the coefficient of x^2 would cause the graphs to reflect and open downward.

4. a) The coordinates of the vertex are (0.75, 6.125) because the graph reaches a maximum of 6.125 when $x = 0.75$.

b) The equation of the axis of symmetry is $x = 0.75$ because the graph is symmetrical about this line.

c) The y-intercept is 5 because $y = 5$ when $x = 0$.

d) The x-intercepts are −1 and 2.5 because $x = -1$ and $x = 2.5$ when $y = 0$.

e) The graph has a maximum value of 6.125.

6.4 Rates of Change in Quadratic Relations

Warm-Up

1. $y = 25$

2. $y = 2x^2 - 4x + 6$ is quadratic

3. You can draw 5 diagonals.

4.

x	y	First Differences
−2	4	
−1	1	−3
0	0	−1
1	1	1

5. 5.3
6. 2
7. $y = 2x^2 - x + 8$; when $x=4$, $y=36$
8. $x = 14$

Practise

1. You can calculate the second differences for the data, and if they are constant then the data represent a quadratic relation.

2. Leon is incorrect because the first differences also have a constant value of 2, so the data must be linear.

3. a)

x	y	First Differences	Second Differences
−3	18		
−2	11	−7	
−1	6	−5	2
0	3	−3	2
1	2	−1	2
2	3	1	2
3	6	3	2

b) The relation is a quadratic relation because the second differences are constant.

c) The shape of the graph forms a parabola because the data form a quadratic relation.

4. a)

x	y	First Differences	Second Differences
−6	10		
−5	4	$4 - 10 = -6$	
−4	0	$0 - 4 = -4$	$-4 - (-6) = 2$
−3	−2	$-2 - 0 = -2$	$-2 - (-4) = 2$
−2	−2	$-2(-2) = 0$	$0 - (-2) = 2$
−1	0	$0(-2) = 2$	$2 - 0 = 2$
0	4	$4 - 0 = 4$	$4 - 2 = 2$
1	10	$10 - 4 = 6$	$6 - 4 = 2$

b) Yes, the relation is quadratic.
Yes, it makes sense that the relation is quadratic because it has an x^2-term.

5. a)

time (s)	height (m)
0	0
1	100
3	250
5	450
6	500
8	600
10	650
13	700
15	675
20	500

b) $y = -4.14x^2 + 107.91x - 5.73$

Chapter 6 Review

1.
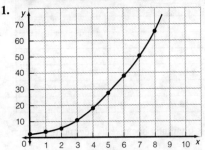

I used a curve of best fit because the points do not form a straight line.

2. a)

r (cm)	A (cm²)
1	3.14
2	12.56
3	28.26
4	50.24
5	78.5
6	113.04
7	153.86
8	200.96
9	254.34
10	314

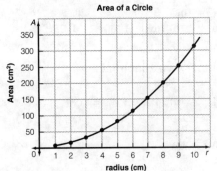

Area of a Circle

3. a) Quadratic because the relation has an x^2-term.
b) Linear because the relation has no x^2-term.
c) Quadratic because the relation has an x^2-term.

4.
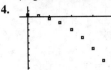

I think the relation is quadratic because the data appears to form a parabola.

5. Coordinates of vertex: $(-2, 0)$
Axis of symmetry: $x = -2$
y-intercept: 4
Minimum value: 0
x-intercept: −2

6.

x	y	First Differences	Second Differences
-3	12		
-2	7	$7 - 12 = -5$	
-1	4	$4 - 7 = -3$	$-3 - (-5) = 2$
0	3	$3 - 4 = -1$	$-1 - (-3) = 2$
1	4	$4 - 3 = 1$	$1 - (-1) = 2$
2	7	$7 - 4 = 3$	$3 - 1 = 2$
3	12	$12 - 5 = 5$	$5 - 3 = 2$

The relation is quadratic because its second differences are constant.

Chapter 7 Quadratic Expressions

Get Set

1. a) monomial
   b) trinomial
   c) monomial
   d) binomial
2. a) $12y$ **b)** $6t^2$ **c)** $-2x$ **d)** $5x$
3. a) $-2x + 3$
   b) $x^2 + 3x + 4$
   c) $9x^2 + 8x - 7$
4. a) $2x - 10$
   b) $10x^2 + 30x$
   c) $-12x^2 - 12x + 6$
   d) $6x^3 + 10x^2$
5. a) 36   **b)** $16x^2$ **c)** $100y^2$ **d)** $25x^2$
6. 288 cm^2

7.1 Multiply Two Binomials

Warm-Up
1. a) 24   **b)** 34
2. a) 8   **b)** 7
3. a) $12x^2 + 8x$
   b) $10x^2 + 30x$
4. a) two
   b) Answers may vary. For example: bicycle
5. 32 m
6. a) $9x + 20$
   b) $3a + 2$

Practise
1. a) Answers may vary. For example: $x + 3$
   b) Answers may vary.
2. a)

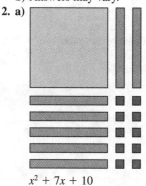

$x^2 + 7x + 10$

b)

$2a^2 + 9a + 4$

3. a) $x^2 + x(3) + 6(x) + (6)(3)$
   $x^2 + 3x + 6x + 18 = x^2 + 9x + 18$
   b) $2x^2 - 20x - 3x + 30 = 2x^2 - 23x + 30$
   c) $7a^2 + 6a - 63a - 54 = 7a^2 - 57a - 54$
4. a)

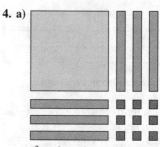

$x^2 + 6x + 9$

   b) Answers may vary. For example: $(x + 3)^2$
   c) square
   d) perfect square trinomial
5. a) Area $= (3x + 5)(x + 5)$
                $= 3x^2 + 5x + 15x + 25$
                $= 3x^2 + 20x + 25$
   b) 112 ft^2
6. $(3x + 2)(x + 2)$
       $= 3x^2 + 6x + 2x + 4$
       $= 3x^2 + 8x + 4$
7. $4x^2 + 11x + 6$

7.2 Common Factoring

Warm-up
1. a) 15   **b)** 6
2. a) Answers may vary. For example: 2, 3, 5
   b) Answers may vary. For example: 2, 3, 4
3. a) $12a - 4a^2 + 2ab$
   b) $-7x + 28y - 42$
4. The opposite process is expanding. Explanations will vary.
5. a) $5   **b)** $0.01
6. a) $-16x - 2$
   b) $5x^2 + 3x + 4$

Practise
1. a) 8   **b)** $2a$ **c)** $2x$
2. a) expanded; 3
   b) factored; 5
   c) expanded; 3
3. a) $3(p - 5)$ Check: $3p^2 - 15$
   b) $3(7x^2 - 3x + 6)$ Check: $21x^2 - 9x + 18$
   c) $6(y^2 + 3y + 10)$ Check: $6y^2 + 18y + 60$
4. Answers may vary. For example: $6n^2 - 3n = 3n(2n - 1)$

5. a) $5x(x + 3)$

b) length: $5x$ m; width: $(x + 3)$ m

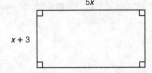

c) 540 m²

d) Perimeter $= 2(5x) + 2(x + 3)$; Area $= 5x(x + 3)$

e) 114 m

6. a) 6   **b)** 9

7.3 Factor a Difference of Squares

Warm-Up

1. a) 32   **b)** 8

2. a) 2, 4   **b)** 4

3. a) $4t^2 - 16$

  b) yes

4. c

5. 122

6. a) $x^2 + 36$ **b)** 45

Practise

1. a) 8^2 **b)** 12^2 **c)** $(3x)^2$

2. a) yes; because first and second terms are perfect squares.

  b) yes; because first and second terms are perfect squares.

  c) no; because second term is not a perfect square

3. a) $(x + 3)(x - 3)$ Check: $x^2 - 9$

  b) $(10 + x)(10 - x)$ Check: $100 - x^2$

  c) $(a + 9)(a - 9)$ Check: $a^2 - 81$

4. a) Answers may vary. Draw a square with side length 6 cm.

  b) $A = 6 \times 6 = 36$ cm²

  c) yes; 6^2 cm² $= 36$ cm²

  d) Answers may vary. $2 \times 2 = 4$ cm²

  e) $36 - 4 = 32$ cm²

  f) $6^2 - 2^2 = 36 - 4 = 32$ cm² or $6^2 - 2^2 = (6 + 2)(6 - 2)$
$$= (8)(4)$$
$$= 32 \text{ cm}^2$$

5. a) $(x + 4)(x - 4)$

  b) Measure a $5 bill to get x; $x = 11$

  c) Substitute $x = 11$ to find the area.
$$(11 + 4)(11 - 4) = (15)(7)$$
$$= 105 \text{ cm}^2$$

  d) $A = 11^2 - 16$
$$= 121 - 16$$
$$= 105 \text{ cm}^2$$

7.4 Factoring Trinomials of the Form $x^2 + bx + c$

Warm Up

1. a) -2 **b)** 68

2. a) 3   **b)** $2x$

3. a) $7x^2 - 14x + 42$

  b) $4b^2 - 28b$

4. Answers may vary.

5. b) 4 h

6. a) $6b^2 - 2b + 13$

  b) 33

Practise

1.

Pair of Integers	Product	Sum
2, 4	8	6
4, 9	36	13
−5, 4	−20	−1
−6, −4	24	−10

2. a)

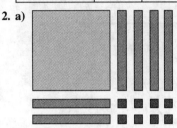

b) length: $x + 4$, width: $x + 2$

c) The expressions for the length and width are the factors of the trinomial expression.

3. a) STEP 1: 3,1;

    STEP 2: $(x + 3)(x + 1)$ Check: $x^2 + 4x + 3$

  b) $(x + 7)(x + 4)$ Check: $x^2 + 11x + 28$

  c) $(x + 5)(x + 4)$ Check: $x^2 + 9x + 20$

4. Answers may vary. While 4 and 2 multiply to give 8, they do not add up to -6. To fix this she should use -4 and -2, which add up to -6 and still multiply to equal 8.

5. a) $A = (x + 7)(x + 1)$

  b) factoring

  c) 160 cm²

6. a) $(x + 3)(x + 3)$. The room is square.

  b) 16 m²

  c)

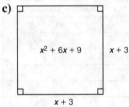

Chapter 7 Review

1. a) $6x^2 + 5x - 4$

  b) $2x^2 + 12x - 14$

  c) $3x^2 - 8x - 3$

  d) $x^2 - 2x + 1$

2. a) $x^2 - 9$

  b) $x^2 + 6x + 9$

  c) Answers may vary.

3. a) No. Completely factored form: $3x(x + 4)$

  b) No. Completely factored form: $6x^2(3x + 1)$

4. a) GCF:2; $2(x^2 + 10)$

  b) GCF:$4xy$; $4xy(x + 2)$

  c) $(x + 12)(x - 12)$

  d) $(x - 7)(x + 2)$

5. a) $25 = 5^2$ **b)** $49 = 7^2$ **c)** $81 = 9^2$

6. a) and **b)** are difference of squares

7. a) $(x + 3)(x - 3)$ Check: $x^2 - 9$

  b) $(x + 4)(x - 4)$ Check: $x^2 - 16$

8. a) length: $x + 6$; width: $x + 1$

  b) The countertop is a rectangle.

  c) 14 ft²

Chapter 8: Represent Quadratic Relations

Get Set

1.

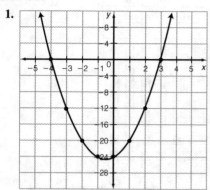

The relation is quadratic.

2. Coordinates of vertex: $(0, -8)$
Equation of axis of symmetry: $x = 0$
x-intercepts: -4 and 4
y-intercepts: -8

3. a) $y = 2$ **b)** $y = 8$
4. a) $x^2 - 8x + 16$ **b)** $x^2 + 3x - 4$
5. a) $4(x^2 - 3)$ **b)** $(x - 5)(x - 2)$

8.1 Interpret Quadratic Relations

Warm-Up

1. $(3, 9)$

2.

x	y	First Differences	Second Differences
-3	20		
-2	13	-7	
-1	8	-5	2
0	5	-3	2
1	4	-1	2
2	5	1	2
3	8	3	2

The relation is quadratic.

3.

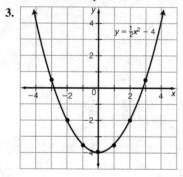

4. a) $y = -x + 3$ **b)** $y = 2x + \dfrac{5}{2}$

---

5. Two lines are parallel if they have the same slope.
For example, $y = x + 2$ and $y = x - 6$ are parallel.
Two lines are perpendicular if their slopes are negative reciprocals of each other. For example, $y = 2x$ and $y = -\dfrac{1}{2}x$ are perpendicular.

6. $3a(a^2 - 5)$
7. $(x - 2)(x + 1)$
8. $y = 8$

Practise: Interpret Quadratic Relations

1. a) 10 m   **b)** 20 m   **c)** 40 m
    d) Yes.   **e)** 35 m

2. a)

time (s)	height (m)
0	210
1	205
2	190
3	165
4	130
5	85
6	30

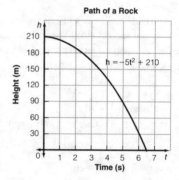

Path of a Rock

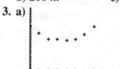

b) 210 m   **c)** 6.5 s   **d)** 157.2 m

3. a)

b) $y = 0.0023x^2 - 0.08x + 2.13$
c) The lowest point is 1.4 m from the ground, this point occurs at a horizontal distance of 17.4 m.
d) The person could stand 8.9 m from either end.

4. Answers may vary. You can determine if a relation is quadratic by graphing with a graphing calculator or by finding the second differences.

5. a)

Fare ($)	Riders	Total Revenue ($)
2.00	240 000	480 000
2.10	230 000	483 000
2.20	220 000	484 000
2.30	210 000	483 000
2.40	200 000	480 000
2.50	190 000	475 000
2.60	180 000	468 000

b)

c) $2.20

d) $484 000

8.2 Represent Quadratic Relations in Different Ways

Warm-Up

1. $(3, -1)$

2.

x	−3	−2	−1	0	1	2	3
y	30	12	0	−6	−6	0	12

3. $(-5, -3)$

4. Enter $y = (x - 2)(x + 1)$ as Y_1 and $y = x^2 - x - 2$ as Y_2 and graph them. Since the two equations are different forms of the same equation only one curve will appear in the window.

5. $(x - 8)(x - 1)$

6. The x-intercepts are −6 and 3.

7. No they are not. When $y = (x - 3)(x + 2)$ is expanded and simplified it is $y = x^2 - x - 6$.

8. The x-intercepts are −6 and −1. The y-intercept is 6.

Practise: Represent Quadratic Relations in Different Ways

1. a) −4 and 7   **b)** −5 and 3   **c)** −4 and 3

2. a) 2   **b)** −4   **c)** −6

3. If the coefficient of the x^2 term is positive, the quadratic relation will have a minimum. If the coefficient of the x^2-term is negative, the quadratic relation will have a maximum.

4. a) $A = x(8 - x)$

b)

x (cm)	0	1	2	3	4	5	6
A (cm²)	0	7	12	15	16	15	12

$x = 4$ will generate the rectangle with the greatest area.

c) The greatest area is 16 cm².

5. a)

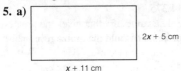

$2x + 5$ cm

$x + 11$ cm

b) $A = (x + 11)(2x + 5) = 2x^2 + 27x + 55$

c) $x = 2$ will produce an area of 117 cm².

6. a) The population will be 50 514.

b) The population was 39 666.

c)

d) The population was least in 1971.

e) The least population was 29 993.

7. a) The d-intercepts are 0 and 40.

b)

distance (m)	0	5	10	15	20	25	30	35	40
height (m)	0	4.375	7.5	9.375	10	9.37	7.5	4.375	0

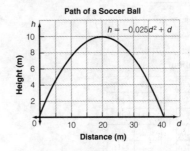

Path of a Soccer Ball

$h = -0.025d^2 + d$

c) The maximum height of the ball is 10 m.

d) The ball traveled 20 m.

8.3 The Quadratic Relation $y = ax^2 + c$

Warm-Up

1. $(2, 3)$

2.

x	−5	−4	−3	−2	−1	0	1	2	3	4	5
y	12	6	2	0	0	2	6	12	20	30	42

3.

x	−5	−4	−3	−2	−1	0	1	2	3	4	5
y	12	6	2	0	0	2	6	12	20	30	42

4.

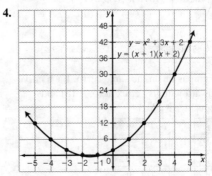

$y = x^2 + 3x + 2$

$y = (x + 1)(x + 2)$

5. Answers may vary. Both graphs lie on the same curve because the two equations are different forms of the same equation.

6. Equations b) and c) are parabolas that open downward because the coefficients of the x^2 terms are negative.

7. $c = 5$

8. $a = 3$

Practise: The Quadratic Relation $y = ax^2 + c$

1. a) iii, ii, i   **b)** ii, iii, i

2.

Quadratic Relation	y-intercept	Maximum or Minimum
a) $y = x^2 + 5$	5	Minimum
b) $y = -\frac{1}{3}x^2 - 7$	−7	Maximum
c) $y = -3x^2 + 27$	27	Maximum
d) $y = \frac{1}{4}x^2 - 1$	−1	Minimum

3. a) none   **b)** none
   c) −3 and 3   **d)** −2 and 2

4. a)

time (s)	depth (m)
0	35
1	31.5
2	21
3	3.5
$\sqrt{10}$	0

b) The tank is 35 m deep.

c) It takes about 3.2 s.

5. a)

x	y
−4	14
−3	0
−2	−10
−1	−16
0	−18
1	−16
2	−10
3	14

x	y
−4	14
−3	0
−2	−10
−1	−16
0	−18
1	−16
2	−10
3	14

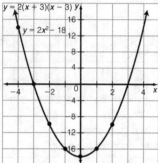

The two graphs lie on the same curve. Each curve opens upward with its vertex at $(0, -18)$ and x-intercepts at -3 and 3.

b)

x	y
−3	−32
−2	−12
−1	0
0	4
1	0
2	−12
3	−32

x	y
−3	−32
−2	−12
−1	0
0	4
1	0
2	−12
3	−32

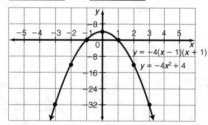

The two graphs lie on the same curve. Each curve opens downward with its vertex at $(0, 4)$ and x-intercepts at -1 and 1.

6. a)

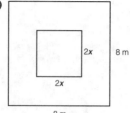

b) 64 m^2 **c)** $4x^2 \text{ m}^2$

d) $A = 64 - 4x^2 \text{ m}^2$

8.4 Solve Problems Involving Quadratic Relations

Warm-Up

1. $(x + 7)(x - 2)$

2.

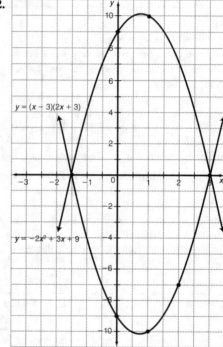

3. $(2h - 9)(2h + 9)$

4. The maximum is 14 375.

5. Answers may vary. The value of x that gives the greatest value for R is the price that would maximize revenue.

6. -18

7. -4 and 4

8. a) 40 s   **b)** 20 s

Practise: Solve Problems Involving Quadratic Relations

1. a)

distance (m)	height (m)
0	3
1	3.54
2	3.96
3	4.26
4	4.44
5	4.5
6	4.44
7	4.26
8	3.96
9	3.54
10	3

The maximum height of the ball was 4.5 m.

b) The horizontal distance travelled when it reaches this maximum height is 5 m.

2. a) 71.7 m **b)** 12.544 m **c)** 3.83 s

3. a) The zeros are at $t = 5.32$ and $t = -0.01$. The zeros represent the times when the ball is on the ground, but since negative time does not exist, the only time the ball is on the ground is at $t = 5.32$ s.

b) 2.65 s

c) 34.74 m

4. a)

time (s)	0	0.5	1	1.5	2	2.5	3
height (m)	1	4.75	6	4.75	1	−5.25	−14

b) 1 m **c)** 6 m; 1 s **d)** 2.1 s

5. a) The cost for running a spring fair.

b) $17

c) $2993.00

Chapter 8 Review

1. a)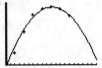

b) 102.1 ft **c)** 23.2 ft **d)** 51.6 ft

2. a)

Price ($)	Number Sold	Revenue ($)
3.50	300	1050.00
3.75	285	1068.75
4.00	270	1080.00
4.25	255	1083.75
4.50	240	1080.00
4.75	225	1068.75
5.00	210	1050.00
5.25	195	1023.75
5.50	180	990.00

b)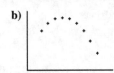

c) $4.25 **d)** $1083.75

3. a) −3, −2 **b)** 0, 8

c) −2, 6 **d)** $0, \dfrac{5}{3}$

4. a) $N = 400 - 8x$

b) $P = 80 + 2x$

c) $R = (400 - 8x)(80 + 2x) = 32\,000 + 160x - 16x^2$

d) $32\,400

e) 360 cars, $90 per car

5. Answers may vary. You can expand and simplify the second equation; if its coefficients are the same as the first equation, the quadratic relations are the same.

6. a)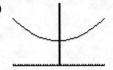

Quadratic Relation	y-Intercept	Maximum or Minimum	x-Intercepts
a) $y = 2x^2 - 32$	−32	Minimum	−4, 4
b) $y = \dfrac{1}{3}x^2 - 3$	−3	Minimum	−3, 3
c) $y = x^2 + 9$	9	Minimum	None
d) $y = -\dfrac{3}{4}x^2 - 5$	−5	Maximum	None

7. a)

b) Minimum value: 4; vertex: (0, 4)

c) y-intercept: 4; x-intercepts: None

8. a) $P = -x^2 + 19x + 150$

b)

c) −6 and 25

d) 950 items should be produced.

e) $240.25

9. a) Answers may vary. Let n be the number of $2 increases.
$$R = (1200 - 60n)(20 + 2n)$$
$$= 24\,000 + 1200n - 120n^2$$

b)

Ticket Price ($)	20	22	24	26	28	30	32	34	36
Tickets Sold (n)	1200	1140	1080	1020	960	900	840	780	720
Revenue ($)	24 000	25 080	25 920	26 520	26 880	27 000	26 880	26 520	25 920

c) $30

d) 900

e) $27 000

Chapter 9 Volume and Surface Area

Get Set

1. 5, 2
$$(5)^2 + (2)^2 = x^2$$
$$25 + 4 = x^2$$
$$29 = x^2$$
$$\sqrt{29} = x$$
$$5.4 \doteq x$$

2. The net has a triangular base and three congruent triangular faces. It is a net of a triangular pyramid.

3. 71 ft; 84 mm; 6000 cm²; 5875.2 in.²

4. 15²; 706.9 ft²

9.1 Volume of Prisms and Pyramids

Warm-Up

1. 6 in.

2. $P = \dfrac{I}{rt}$

3. $t = \sqrt{\dfrac{d}{a}}$

4. Answers may vary. To find the volume of a cup to see how much liquid it can hold.

5. $y = 11$

6. $A = -46$

Practise

1. $A = 85 \times 12$
$= 1020$ cm^2; 1020 cm^2
$V = 1020 \times 15$
$= 15\ 300$ cm^3; 15 300 cm^3

2. $A = \dfrac{1}{2}(18)(22)$
$= 198$ in.^{2}; 198 in.^{2}
$V = 198 \times 44$
$= 8712$ in.^{3}; 8712 in.^{3}

3. $A = 39 \times 20$
$= 780$ ft^2; 780 ft^2
$V = \dfrac{1}{3}(780)(70)$
$= 18\ 200$ ft^3; 18 200 ft^3

4. $0.6^2 + h^2 = 1.2^2$
$h^2 = 1.2^2 - 0.6^2$
$h^2 = 1.44 - 0.36$
$h^2 = 1.08^2$
$h^2 \doteq 1.04$ m^2

$A = \dfrac{1}{2}(1.2)(1.04)$
$= 0.624$ m^2; 0.624 m^2
$V = (0.624)(6.3)$
$= 3.931$ m^3; 3.931 m^3

5. 400 cm^3

9.2 Surface Area of Prisms and Pyramids

Warm-Up

1. Answers may vary.

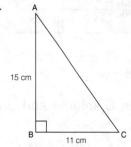

$AC \doteq 18.6$ cm

2. Answers may vary. To find the amount of wrapping paper needed to wrap a gift box.
To find the amount of cardboard needed to create a box.

3. a) $h = \dfrac{A}{b}$ **b)** $r = \dfrac{C}{2\pi}$

4. a) $x = 55$ **b)** $y = 36$

5. A cube

6. A square-based pyramid.

7. b)

8. Answers may vary. No, since the triangle is not a right triangle.

Practise

1. Answers may vary.

2. $A = 15 \times 12$
$= 180$ cm^2
$A = 15 \times 85$
$= 1275$ cm^2
$A = 85 \times 12$
$= 1020$ cm^2
$A_{\text{Surface}} = 2(180) + 2(1275) + 2(1020)$
$= 4950$ cm^2; 4950 cm^2

3. Answers may vary.

14 cm

20 cm

4. STEP 1:
$h^2 + 7^2 = 20^2$
$h^2 = 20^2 - 7^2$
$h^2 = \sqrt{20^2 - 7^2}$
$h \doteq 18.73$
STEP 2:
$A \doteq \dfrac{1}{2}(14)(18.73)$
$= 131.1$ cm^2
STEP 3: SA of triangle faces
$A \doteq 4(131.1)$
$\doteq 524.4$ cm^2
SA of base $= 14 \times 4$
$= 196$ cm^2
Total SA is $524.4 + 196 = 720.4$ cm^2

5. a) 90 m^2 **b)** \$1255.50

9.3 Surface Area and Volume of Cylinders

Warm-Up

1. Answers may vary. Canned food; cups

2. πr^2

3. c)

4. 3.14

5. a) 105 yd   **b)** 185 mm   **c)** 223 cm^2 **d)** 3 ft^3

6. a) $n = \dfrac{PV}{RT}$ **b)** $w = \dfrac{P - 2l}{2}$

7. 7920 m^3

8. 41 in.^{2}

Practise

1. $2\pi (20)^2 + 2\pi (20)(65) \doteq 2512 + 8168$
$\doteq 10\ 676$; 10 676 cm^2

2. 21; $2\pi (10.5)^2 + 2\pi (10.5) \doteq 758.3$; 758.3 cm^2

3. $\pi(6)^2 (7.2) \doteq 813.9$; 813.9 m^3

4. 1.44; $\pi(0.72)^2 (42) \doteq 68.4$; 68.4 m^3

5. a) $\pi(4)^2 (18) \doteq 904.3$; 904.3 cm^3
b) $\pi(1.5)^2 (18) \doteq 127.2$; 127.2 cm^3
c) 777.1 cm^3

6. Answers may vary. You would need more paint after it was hollowed out because the area of the inside surface is greater than the area of the circle openings.

9.4 Volume of Cones and Spheres

Warm-Up

1. No, it will be 8 times the volume.
2. Answers may vary. pylon; ice-cream cone
3. 46 cm
4. Answers may vary. orange; the Sun
5. **a)** 42 000 m
   b) 3520 mm
   c) 573 000 mm^3
   d) 1250 ft^2
6. **a)** $I = \sqrt{\dfrac{P}{R}}$ **b)** $V = \dfrac{m}{D}$
7. **a)** 1727 in.^{3} **b)** 7033.6 cm^2
8. 10.5

Practise

1. **a)** $\dfrac{1}{3}\pi(14)^2(22)$
   $\doteq 4513.2$; 4513.2 cm^3

   b) 24; $V = \dfrac{1}{3}\pi r^2 h$
   $= \dfrac{1}{3}\pi(5)^2(24)$
   $= 628$; 628 in.^{3}

2. **a)** $\dfrac{4}{3}\pi(18)^3$
   $\doteq 24\ 416.6$; 24 416.6 m^3

   b) diameter = 6 cm; radius = 3 cm
   $V = \dfrac{4}{3}\pi r^2$
   $= \dfrac{4}{3}\pi(3)^3$
   $\doteq 113.0$; 113.0 cm^3

3. **a)** $\dfrac{1}{3}\pi(18)^2(100)$
   $\doteq 33912$; 33912 in.^{3}

   b) $r = \sqrt[3]{\dfrac{3V}{4\pi}}$
   $r = \sqrt[3]{\dfrac{3 \times 16\ 956}{4\pi}}$
   $= \sqrt[3]{4050}$
   $\doteq 15.9$ in.

   c) 31.8 in.
4. **a)** 9 cm   **b)** 3052.1 cm^3

9.5 Solve Problems Involving Surface Area and Volume

Warm-Up

1. **a)** 93 ft   **b)** 4.2 mm
   c) 0.2276 m^2 **d)** 1674 ft^3
2. Answers may vary. Regina is correct, Seema is not. The area of the base does not change when the height is doubled.
3. 36 in.^{3}
4. 288 in.^{3}
5. **a)** $h = \dfrac{SA - 2\pi r^2}{2\pi r}$ **b)** $c = \sqrt{\dfrac{E}{m}}$
6. $x = 3$

Practise

1. **a)** cylinders: 175.8 cm^3;
   rectangular prism: 2240 cm^3
   b) Sphere A: 14 130 in.^{3}
   Sphere B: 65 416.7 in.^{3}
   Sphere C: 113 040 in.^{3}
2. Area of back rectangle = 12×8
   $= 96$
   Area of front = $12 \times 8 - \pi(1.5)^2$
   $= 88.9$
   Area of 2 sides = $2 \times 8 \times 8$
   $= 128$
   Area of base = 12×8
   $= 96$
   Area of front and back triangles = $\dfrac{1}{2} \times 12 \times 5$
   $= 30$
   Area of roof = $2 \times 8 \times 7.8$
   $= 124.8$
   Total surface area to be painted = 453.7 in.^{2}
3. **a)** Answers may vary.

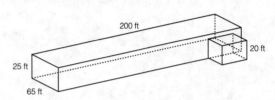

   b) 333 000 ft^3

Chapter 9 Review

1. $V = l \times w \times h$
   $= 60 \times 14 \times 22$
   $= 18\ 480$ cm^3
2. $V = \dfrac{1}{3}$ area of base $\times$ height
   $= \dfrac{1}{3} \times 40 \times 20 \times 70$
   $= 18\ 666.7$ ft^3
3. 5,8; $A = 5 \times 8$
   $= 40$
   5,9; $A = 5 \times 9$
   $= 45$
   8,9; $A = 8 \times 9$
   $= 72$
   $A_{Surface} = 2(40) + 2(45) + 2(72)$
   $= 314$; 314 yd^2
4. Circular top SA = 78.5 in.^{2}
   Side SA = 439.6 in
   Cylinder SA = 596.6 in.^{2}
   Cylinder V = 1099 in.^{3}
5. **a)** 0.5 yd^3 **b)** 670 637.9 cm^3

9.4 Solve Problems Involving Surface Area and Volume, textbook pages 398-405

6. **a)** 2253 in.^{2} **b)** 7173 in.^{3}